Health Care Economics: The Market for Physician Services

European University Studies

Europäische Hochschulschriften
Publications Universitaires Européennes

Series V
Economics and Management

Reihe V   Série V
Volks- und Betriebswirtschaft
Sciences économiques, gestion d'entreprise

Vol./Bd. 2853

PETER LANG

Frankfurt am Main · Berlin · Bern · Bruxelles · New York · Oxford · Wien

Franz Benstetter

Health Care Economics: The Market for Physician Services

PETER LANG
Europäischer Verlag der Wissenschaften

Die Deutsche Bibliothek - CIP-Einheitsaufnahme

Benstetter, Franz :

Health care economics: the market for physician services /
Franz Benstetter. - Frankfurt am Main ; Berlin ; Bern ; Bruxelles ;
New York ; Oxford ; Wien : Lang, 2002
 (European university studies : Ser. 05, Economics and
 Management ; Vol. 2853)
 Zugl.: München, Univ., Diss., 2001
 ISBN 3-631-39078-5

Gedruckt mit Unterstützung der
Hans-Böckler-Stiftung.

Gedruckt auf alterungsbeständigem,
säurefreiem Papier.

D 19
ISSN 0531-7339
ISBN 3-631-39078-5
US-ISBN 0-8204-5477-X

© Peter Lang GmbH
Europäischer Verlag der Wissenschaften
Frankfurt am Main 2002
All rights reserved.

Printed in Germany 1 2 3 4 5   7

www.peterlang.de

To my parents

and

to Erika

Acknowledgements

I would like to thank a number of people who supported me in writing this thesis. First of all, I am very grateful to my supervisor Monika Schnitzer for her support and encouragement. Also, I would like to thank Achim Wambach, the co-author of Chapter 4 and 5, for his stimulation of precise economic thinking. In addition my thanks go to Patrick D'Souza, Clement Krouse, Florian Meise, Marcus Mirbach, Günther Oppermann, Sven Rady, Ray Rees (who also acted as co-referee), Michael Reutter, Klaus M. Schmidt, Stefan Schubert and Konrad Stahl for helpful comments and suggestions. Moreover I am very grateful to Marcus Mirbach, who constantly helped me to improve my LaTeX-skills. Last but not least I would like to thank the Hans-Böckler foundation, especially Werner Fiedler and his team, for support and the Central Research Institute of Ambulatory Health Care in Germany for providing data.

Contents

List of Tables

List of Figures

Chapter 1

Introduction

The market for physician services is a quantitatively important market in almost all industrialized economies. Total expenditure for health care in the United States in 1999 amounted to 1.2 trillion U.S. \$, or 13.7 % of gross domestic product (GDP). In the same year 229.5 billion U.S. \$ have been spent on outpatient care[1] on top physicians and dentists (OECD, 2000).

Also important to note is the steady increase in medical expenditures observed since 1980 (see Table 1.1). Germany is one of the EU countries with the largest share of its GDP on health care (10.6 percent in 1998).[2] In the 80s the growth of health expenditure approximated the growth in the economy, but during the last ten years the growth in health expenditure has become greater. The costs of unification, the aging population and the introduction of new technologies have been listed as some of the possible reasons behind this increase.[3]

Consequently it is not surprising that politicians have tried to contain and steer these costs through various health care reforms, depending on the

---

[1]The term "outpatient care" refers to medical services that can be provided outside of the inpatient wards of a hospital. A synonym for outpatient care is the term ambulatory care.

[2]The total expenditure on health care per capita are shown in Figure A.1 in Appendix A.

[3]For details see Kanavos and Yfantopoulos (1999) and Altenstetter (1999).

Table 1.1: International comparison of health expenditure

	Total Expenditure for health 1998 in percentage of gross domestic product	Value change since 1980 in %
U.S.A.	13,6	52,8
Germany	10,6	20,5
Switzerland	10,4	50,7
France	9,6	29,7
Canada	9,5	31,9
Belgium	8,8	37,5
Netherlands	8,6	3,6
Italy	8,4	20,0
Finland	6,9	7,8
Great Britain	6,7	17,5

Source: OECD (2000)

constitutional and institutional specialties of the various national health care markets.[4] In the United States, for instance, since the 1980s the health care markets have been dominated by two major trends: Enormous growth in managed care[5] and most recently, a strong movement towards consolidation, both horizontally and vertically (Gaynor and Haas-Wilson, 1999). Both of these developments are characterized by changes in the nature of contracts between physicians and health plans.

Germany has tried to reform its health care system several times during the '90s.[6] In 1993 the German market for physician services switched from the fee-for-service reimbursement system to a system with an ex-ante

---

[4]Cost containment is generally defined as the control of inefficiencies in the consumption, allocation, or production of health care services that contribute to higher than necessary costs.

[5]The term managed care generally denotes explicit efforts by insurers to influence utilization through their relationships with providers. Therefore managed care is any system of health payment or delivery arrangements where the health plan attempts to control or coordinate use of health services by its "enrolled members" in order to contain health expenditures, improve quality, or both.

[6]The German health care reforms of the '90s are listed in Section 2.2.

fixed budget. Currently, the health care system undergoes a new round of restructuring by the proposed introduction of a so-called "global budget": To stabilize the share of health care expenditure on the gross domestic product and the contribution rate of employees and employers[7] to the statutory sickness funds, the total expenditures to all suppliers in the health care market will be fixed.

All these reforms have had only minor effects on the overall expenditures for health care, which indicates that the activities lacked the necessary understanding of the health care market. Thus, to implement successful health care reforms it is necessary to understand one of the fundamental aspects of the system, namely the market for physician services:

In most countries like the U.S.A. and Germany this market for physician services is of intense policy interest due to its size and its pivotal situation in health care. In Germany in 1997, total expenditure for physician services accounted for about 65 billion Deutsch Marks and for dental services for about 42 billion Deutsch Marks.[8] The pivotal situation of this market for physician services lies

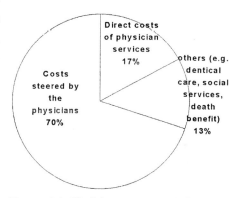

Figure 1.1: Health care costs influenced by physicians (in percentage), Source: Bundesministerium für Gesundheit (2000c)

in the fact that for instance in Germany nearly 90 % of all treatments are initialized by the physicians: Physician do not only treat people in ambulatory care, but they also steer costs when they prescribe pharmaceuticals and

---

[7]Generally these contributions to the statutory sickness funds are jointly paid by employers and employees.
[8]See e.g. OECD (2000).

admit patients to the hospital or to a cure.[9] For 1999 this is shown for total expenditures for statutory health care in Figure 1.1 and Figure 1.2.

Due to the fact that utilization of resources in health care is predominantly controlled by physicians, a thorough understanding of remuneration systems in these markets, especially of the influence of reimbursement contracting on physicians' behavior, is essential for understanding the potential effects of policy interventions and for predicting the long run viability of a health care system.

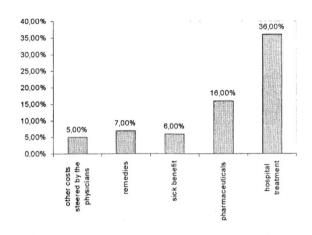

Figure 1.2: Structure of expenditures steered by physicians, Source: Bundesministerium für Gesundheit (2000c)

There are key characteristics of the health care market that impede this understanding. The crucial feature of this market is information or better the lack of information. As the patient does not know his true condition or the technology of producing health from health care, the physician has an incentive to deviate from his agency responsibility for his own advantage by inducing demand.

As an empirical fact we observe that physicians act differently under the various remuneration systems, which leads to a number of questions: How does reimbursement contracting effect physicians' practices, such as their

---

[9]For details see Leiter, Loest, and Thielscher (1997).

number of treatments (work load) and their income? How do reimbursement systems effect prices of treatments?

This is the starting point for the present thesis, which investigates and compares alternative physician reimbursement schemes and their implications for health care reforms. This is done by a positive analysis. An understanding of the interactions in the markets for physician services and of the incentive effects of policy proposals can inform the debate over policies with the goal to regulate these interactions.

In addition to giving an overview on the German health care system and of the modelling of physician behavior in the literature, the thesis investigates supplier induced demand in a formal version. It makes two further major contributions:

1. It contributes to the understanding of a remuneration system with a fixed budget. This thesis shows that a market for physician services with a fixed reimbursement budget involves - compared to a fee-for-service remuneration system - a severe coordination problem, which potentially leads to the "treadmill effect" where physicians increase their number of treatments. In 1993 the switch from the fee for service reimbursement system to the payment system with a fixed budget in Germany led to the following three interesting observations: First, the price determined ex post in this prospective remuneration system dropped significantly. Second, a reduced average income of physicians could be observed. And third, also the number of physicians' treatments increased. The analysis not only suggests one possible explanation for the three observations, but also suggests that the introduction of a specific mechanism of a price floor into the prospective market for physician services could solve this coordination problem. As regulation authorities in the health care market also face the problem of finding the right overall level of reimbursement for physician services, it will also be shown that a budget system can be efficiency enhancing

if market entry is possible. This investigation is in line with the strand of literature, where physicians can induce demand directly. However, compared to the previous literature the presented model does not assume that inducement is limited via an exogenous target income or via a possible negative utility, but by (convex) costs instead. In addition, strategic aspects (in the presented case induced through a fixed budget) have not been investigated so far. Further, policy proposals to solve the coordination problem in the German market for physician services are presented in a rigorous analytical framework. Finally, this thesis also detects - often incorrectly - commonplaces in the German debate about remuneration systems for health care providers. For instance it is argued that the switch from a fee-for-service system to a reimbursement system with a fixed total budget has put the physicians in a prisoners dilemma which lead to an increase in the number of treatments. We show that this view is not correct. For the institutional setting of German primary physician services we will provide evidence which is consistent with the theoretical predictions of this contribution.

2. In our second contribution to the market for physician services the distribution of risks between insurers and physicians in different remuneration systems is analyzed. Especially the remuneration systems fee-for-service, fee-per-capita and the budget system are compared with respect to aggregate risk (of the population to get ill) and with respect to idiosyncratic risk (risk per doctor). It is shown that the popular argument that the budget system - compared to the fee-for-service system - shifts the morbidity risk (aggregate risk) from the insurer to the physician holds only in the case where variable costs are more uncertain than income. Further, if the riskiness in the number of patients differs between different groups of physicians, then in a budget system (but not in a price or capitation system) there are spillover effects between groups of physicians which are investigated. This helps to explain why

for example in Germany some treatments are remunerated outside the budget system and why some groups of physicians are more strongly opposed to the budget system than others.

This thesis is organized as follows: Chapter 2 provides information about structure and trends in the German health care market as observations in the German health care market are the basis for the investigated issues in health care. Because of the pivotal situation of the market for physician services, Chapter 3 surveys important parts of the literature on physician services, especially supplier-induced demand. In Chapter 4 a model of physician choice is presented, in which strategic interaction in the market for physician services (through a fixed budget) are investigated and where solutions to the analyzed coordination problem are derived. Chapter 5 shows how aggregate uncertainty and idiosyncratic risk per doctor about the number of treatments influences the physicians' preferences for the different reimbursement systems. In Chapter 6 empirical evidence for the German market for physician services is given. Chapter 7 concludes the thesis and summarizes the findings.

Chapter 2

The Structure of the German Health Care System

As the German market for physician services is embedded in the German health care system through its relationship to other key actors, it is necessary to first discuss some major institutions and mechanism of the German health care system. This system is organized as a network and includes governmental and non-governmental institutions and firms, such as public (statutory) health insurance funds and national health associations like the federal association of panel doctors. More than 50 percent of all of the tasks carried out by German health care system are financed by the statutory health insurance (SHI), which underlines its central position in the health care system.[10] Other major institutions providing services and benefits in health care to the population are the long-term care insurance, the statutory pension insurance and the statutory accident insurance. The flows of financing in German health care are shown in Figure 2.1.

The regulators in the German health system are the Ministries of Labor and Social Affairs in the states and the federal Ministry of Health. On the one hand, the government specifies the legal framework for the SHI system, and

---

[10]See Bundesministerium für Gesundheit (2000c).

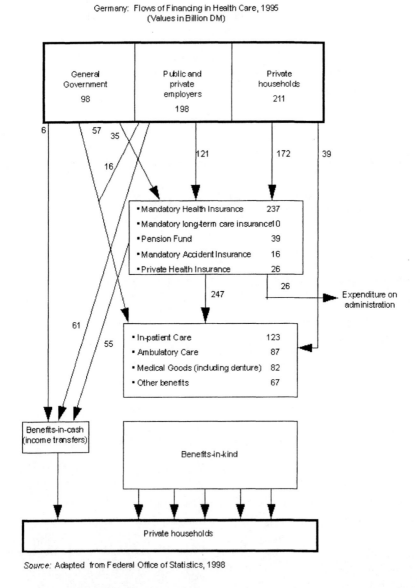

Figure 2.1: Financial flows in the German market for physician services 1995

the major part of sickness funds' benefits are provided according to this legal framework. On the other hand, the insurance providers are self-governing and possess the administrative autonomy to negotiate with the medical and hospital associations as the providers of health care services and purchasers (mainly the sickness funds) are strictly separated.

Because of its important role for the remuneration of health care providers, the institutional structure and management of the German health care system will be briefly described.[11] First, for a better understanding of the situation of the German health care system, Section 2.1 describes the major health services purchasers. Section 2.2 gives an overview of reforms which had been important for cost containment especially in the market for physician services which characterizes the changes in the nature of contracts between providers and health plans. Finally, in Section 2.3 we highlight the specifics of the German physician remuneration and the contracting relationships of the physicians being the institutional foundation for the more in-depth analysis of physician behavior under a complex reimbursement system.

2.1 Financing and Coverage of the Health Care System

Statutory Sickness Funds

Approximately 90 percent of the German population are insured with one of the compulsory public health insurance funds.[12] This is the case with employees with a salary not exceeding a certain limit, set by the federal government at the beginning of each year.[13] Besides these employees below

---

[11]For a brief overview of the main organizational interrelationships of all major actors in the German health care system see Figure A.2.

[12]See Federal Association of Panel Doctors (1999, Table G1).

[13]In the year 2000 the ceiling stood at a gross income of DM 6,450 per month in the Old Länder and DM 5,325 in the New Länder, see Bundesministerium für Gesundheit (2000c).

a certain income level also students, people in training (apprenticeship), farmers, unemployed and people in need are insured as mandatory members by the public health insurance funds as well as non-employed member spouses and children of all these groups, who are not employed. If a person exceeds the income ceiling he can stay in the public health system as a voluntary member, if he was a member directly before. After retirement, senior citizens generally remain members in the public health insurance funds. In 1999 out of the 71.3 million people[14] insured in the public health insurance funds, 29.3 million people were mandatory members, 15.3 million members in retirement, 6.3 million voluntarily insured members and 20.4 million family dependents.[15]

The contributions of the mandatory members are calculated as a percentage of the member's gross wage or gross salary.[16] In principle, employee and employer share the health insurance contribution by each paying fifty percent. Neither individual health risk, age nor sex have impact on the contribution level. The right to get medical benefits and services is independent of the size of the contribution.

The compulsory tasks performed by the statutory health insurance are prevention, early detection and treatment of disease, medical rehabilitation, payment of sickness benefits, providing pregnancy and maternity benefits and health promotion. Since April 1995 the financing and benefits to persons in need of intensive long-term care were transferred from the benefit catalogue of the SHI to the long-term care insurance.

In January 2000, 51.1 million members[17] were insured in 541 autonomous sickness funds in Germany. With 20 million members the general health insurance funds have the largest membership and geographically cover the whole country with their autonomous Länder-based funds (Allgemeine Ortskrankenkassen). Anybody not choosing to join another insurance is

---

[14]58.8 million in the Old Länder and 12.5 million in the New Länder

[15]See Bundesministerium für Gesundheit (2000c).

[16]For voluntary members the assessment of contribution is only up to the mentioned above ceiling.

[17]Family dependents are not included in the term "member".

automatically insured with the general health insurance funds. With 18.7 Million members the substitute health insurance funds (Ersatzkassen) are the second largest group of public insurers and are operating nationwide. The third group includes the insurance funds based on corporations or industry.[18] Until 1995, most of the population were assigned by law to specific health insurance funds. Only some of the insured - in particular the salaried employees - had some possibilities to choose. Today, in principle, every member, irrespective of his profession or employer can choose from a variety of public health insurance funds.

Private Health Insurers

Additionally to the statutory sickness funds there are private health insurance funds, where about 10 percent of the German population is insured.[19] These private funds cover employees above the ceiling described above who choose a private health insurer, self-employed persons and civil servants to whom the government pays financial assistance (called "Beihilfe"). Contrary to the members of the statutory sickness funds, the members of the private insurance funds pay the health care providers directly. Afterwards, depending on the insurance contract, the members are partially or fully reimbursed by the insurer.

In 1998 there had been 94 private health insurers in Germany, where 52 out of 57 nationwide operating insurers are joined in the Association of Private Insurers. These companies present the whole private health insurance market as 99,95 percent of the yield is contributed by these companies.

---

[18]To this third group of public insurances belong the employees' insurance funds established by large manufacturing corporations (Betriebskrankenkassen), the tradesmen's insurance funds (Innungskrankenkassen), the miners' insurance funds (Bundesknappschaft), the agricultural insurance fund (Landwirtschaftliche Krankenkasse) and the sailors' insurance fund (Seekrankenkasse). For a detailed analysis of the membership to the various groups of statutory insurances, separated for the Old and for the New Länder see Bundesministerium für Gesundheit (2000c, Table 10.6.).

[19]For details see Verband der privaten Krankenversicherung e.V. (2000) and Federal Association of Panel Doctors (1999, Table G1).

The remaining smaller companies offer mainly supplementary insurance and operate on a local basis.[20]

2.2   Recent Major Reforms in the German Health Care Market

As in almost any other country, many health care reforms have passed in the last two decades to stop rising health care expenditures.

The basic idea behind German-style cost containment was an income-oriented expenditure policy to guarantee stable contribution rates. This was an important objective in a time of economic restructuring (i.e. the German reunification and growing international competition), since the contributions which cover ambulatory care, pharmaceuticals and hospital care (with the exclusion of hospital investment and some dental treatment) are jointly paid by employers and employees. Rising contribution rates therefore became a question of international competitiveness.[21]

This line of thought and the extraordinary task of including the eastern part of the country after the reunification[22] have increased the pressure on the system and contributed to the increasing speed of health care reform legislation in the 1990. The Reform acts are listed in Table 2.1.

A series of cost-containment acts employing various tools were used, including:

- budgets for sectors or individual providers;

- reference-price setting for pharmaceuticals;

- restrictions on high cost technology equipment;

---

[20]See Verband der privaten Krankenversicherung e.V. (2000)
[21]See Sachverständigenrat für die Konzertierte Aktion im Gesundheitswesen (1997).
[22]See Sachverständigenrat für die Konzertierte Aktion im Gesundheitswesen (1997).

- restrained number of ambulatory care physicians per geographic planning region;

- increased co-payments (both in terms of level and number of services);

- introduction of a risk compensation scheme to redistribute contributions among sickness funds.

The Health Reform Act[23] introduced reference prices and a negativlist (based on inefficiencies) for pharmaceuticals, public committees to regulate expensive technologies and in-home long-term care benefits.

Table 2.1: Major health care reforms acts since 1988

Reform act	Year passed
Health care Reform Act 1989 ("First step")	1988
Health Care Structure Act 1993 ("Second step")	1992
Health Insurance Contribution Rate Exoneration Act	1996
1st & 2nd Statutory Health Insurance Restructuring Act ("Third step")	1997
Act to Strengthen Solidarity in Statutory Health Insurance	1998
Reform Act of Statutory Health Insurance 2000	1999

The Health Care Insurance Contribution Rate Exoneration Act and, more explicitly, the First and Second Statutory Health Insurance Restructuring Acts represented a shift from cost-containment to a possible expansion of private payments. These laws included increased co-payments for inpatient care, rehabilitative care, pharmaceuticals, medical aids, and transportation (to the hospital); an exclusion of young persons from certain dental benefits during 1997 and 1998 (mainly crowns and dentures) but also the privatization of the relationship between dentists and patients for these treatments; and

---

[23]Bundesgesetzblatt (1988)

an annual flat premium of DM 20 for the restoration and repair of hospitals which had to be paid entirely by the insured.[24]

The Act to Strengthen Solidarity in Statutory Health Insurance reversed some of these changes since they were perceived by the new government to violate the basic principles of the statutory health insurance system, namely uniform availability of benefits, equally shared contributions between employers and employees, financing depending only on income and not on risk or service utilization, and the provision of services as benefits-in-kind.[25]

The Reform Act of Statutory Health Insurance 2000 does not have one central theme but rather tries to address a range of (perceived) weaknesses of the system by strengthening primary care, opening opportunities for overcoming the strict separation between the outpatient and inpatient care sectors, introducing new requirements for health technology assessment and quality assurance, as well as supporting patients' rights. In addition, the payment system for hospital care will be changed.[26]

The key reform for this thesis was the Health Care Structure Act, which came into force on January 1, 1993. The act pursued three strategies:[27]

- more competition to enhance efficiency, especially between different sickness funds and in the hospital sector (e.g. financial adjustments to reduce the income and risk gaps among sickness funds);

- tighter restrictions on the number of outpatient care physicians;

- increased emphasis on clear-cut cost-containment measures, especially by the introduction of legally set fixed budgets for the major sectors of health care.

---

[24]For details see Bundesgesetzblatt (1997a) and Bundesgesetzblatt (1997b).

[25]See European Observatory on Health Care Systems (2000).

[26]See e.g. Bundesministerium für Gesundheit (2000a), HWWA - Institut für Wirtschaftsforschung (1999) and Bundesministerium für Gesundheit (2000b).

[27]For details see Bundesgesetzblatt (1992).

This third strategy of the Health Care Structure Act was originally limited until 1995, but was expanded. In June 1997, the associations of panel doctors introduced the so-called "Practice-budget" into the market for physician services in agreement with the public sickness funds. Consequently the reimbursement system for physicians shifted from a pure budget to a modified system, which includes a maximal number of treatments per physician. This maximal number depends on the calculated average treatments per group of physicians and on the age of the patients.

In 1998 with the modification of the § 85 of the 5th Social Welfare Legislation Act (SGB V) in the 2nd Statutory Health Insurance Restructuring Act the so-called "Regelleistungsvolumen" had been made possible. The Bavarian association of panel doctors together with the primary sickness funds were the first who implemented this modification of the point system where a certain point value was guaranteed, however only for a limited predetermined number of treatments, which also depends on previous patient visits per physician. Compared to the "Practice-budget" treatments above this predetermined number had been reimbursed, but only by a downward graduated point value.[28]

Because of the introduction of the Act to Strengthen Solidarity in Statutory Health Insurance ("Vorschaltgesetz") in January 1999, this system could not be tested furthermore.

In the current German debate the question remains on the top of the agenda whether a point system with a fixed budget, where each treatment has a certain amount of points serves as the adequate reimbursement scheme for physicians and other health care providers.[29]

---

[28]See e.g. Kassenärztliche Vereinigung Bayerns (1998).

[29]Alternative reimbursement systems are among others the price-system, where each treatment is reimbursed by a fixed price - our benchmark case fee-for-service - and the capitation system, where each doctor receives a fixed amount per capita.

2.3   The German Market for Physician Services

Until the '90s the public health system paid physicians on a fee-for-service basis. Since the health care reform in 1993 we find administered caps on the total budget for outpatient care. Right now the costs may not rise faster than labor's share in national income. In 1998, outpatient care for physicians[30] accounted for about 17,4 percent (more than 40 billion Deutsch Marks) of the total health care bill paid by the statutory funds in Germany (see Federal Association of Panel Doctors (1999, Table G3)). This segment outpatient care is largely made up of the services provided by doctors and dentists with their own practices. At the end of 1998, there were about 125,000 practicing physicians in various fields in outpatient care and about 60,000 dentists in Germany.[31]

According to the 5th Social Welfare Legislation Act (SGB V), outpatient medical care for patients insured under a statutory health insurance fund will be reimbursed only if treated by physicians bound to the statutory insurance funds by contract. Over 95% of all general practitioners are on contract with the statutory health insurance funds; the remaining 5% treat only privately insured patients. The German government merely defines the legislative framework for the bargaining process between the medical associations of panel doctors and the statutory sickness funds and mandates these insurance funds and their contract doctors to cooperate. These participating physicians are organized in regional associations of panel doctors and with the federal association, the umbrella organization. The regional associations and the national or regional sickness funds are self-controlled bodies. In the German system for outpatient care there is no direct financial flow or contract relationship between the individual participating

---

[30]Outpatient care for dentists accounted for about 10 percent of the total health care bill.

[31]See Federal Association of Panel Doctors (1999, Table A1) and HypoVereinsbank (1999) for dentists.

physicians[32] and the sickness funds. Instead, there are contracts between the regional associations of panel doctors and the sickness funds on the one hand, and the regional doctors associations and the participating physicians on the other. Therefore the reimbursement associations act as an intermediare for the reimbursement flows with their respective contract parties. Furthermore, primary physician service in the German outpatient market is assured by this institution of panel doctors.[33] Physicians in outpatient care being in contract with the statutory health insurance funds via the associations of panel doctors are obliged to provide patients with all "necessary" services, which are specified in the funds' performance spectrum, in the context and framework of legally binding contracts and government directives. Legally, the relationship between the insured and his doctor is a service contract under the Civil Code (Bürgerliches Gesetzbuch, BGB). Following the above logic, the insured by statutory health insurance funds neither pay physicians directly for treatment nor receive the physicians' bills for treatment.[34] The individual contractual relationships between physicians, associations of panel doctors, statutory health insurance funds and patients can be studied in the following Figure 2.2.

The remuneration for physician services is organized in two major steps. In the first step the statutory sickness funds make total payments to the associations of panel doctors. Usually this total payment is negotiated between the insurance funds and the associations of panel doctors as a capitation per member or per insured person or is fixed by legislation.[35] The

---

[32]Since 1999 a new reform act allows to a certain degree for contracts between health care providers and sickness funds to improve cooperation of general practitioners, ambulatory specialists and hospitals. However, there are only a few pilot projects which take usually the form of gatekeeping models. Gatekeepers are primary care physicians who must authorize all medical services (for instance hospitalizations, diagnostic work-ups, and speciality referrals) for an insurance member, unless there is an emergency.

[33]This institution is also called association of social health insurance physicians.

[34]In contrast, privately insured patients are directly billed by their physicians, pay the physicians directly and forward the original invoices to the health insurance for reimbursement.

[35]As mentioned before besides mandatory members also their spouses and children are insured in the compulsory public health insurance funds.

The collective contract regulates the relationship between statutory sickness funds and the renumeration distribution regulates the relationship between physicians and their association of panel doctors:

Figure 2.2: The contractual relationships in the German market for physician services

capitation value covers all treatments carried out by the physicians who are affiliated to the outpatient market and varies between general and substitute health insurance funds.

In the second step the regional associations of panel doctors disburse these total payments to the panel doctors according to a uniform evaluation standard[36] and additional statutes.[37] The uniform evaluation standard allocates a specific number of points to some 2,000 outpatient services which can be provided by physicians for remuneration within the statutory health insurance system. Right now the prices are determined ex post by adjusting the monetary value of a point on the fee schedule to account for differences between the actual and expected volume of services. The uniform evaluation

---

[36]In Germany known as the "EBM" (Einheitlicher Bewertungsmaßstab).

[37]The regional associations that administer the reimbursement can exert some influence via separate individual budgets by applying fee distribution criteria.

standard contains all medical treatments which are approved by the Federal Committee of Physicians and Sickness Funds.

One subcommittee of this federal level committee is in charge for the technology assessment of diagnostic and treatment procedures (§ 135 SGB V). Until July 1997 new technologies could be proposed by either a federal sickness funds' association or by the Federal Association of Panel Doctors. According to an outlined set of criteria new procedures could be accepted if they were approved to be necessary from a physician's perspective and if a reasonable statistical investigation could be obtained.[38] However, with rising critiques that these procedures could be easily influenced by questionable scientific evidence, in 1997 stronger guidelines were introduced, taking besides medical necessity also benefit and efficiency of the proposed technology into account. Since 1997 this committee is called the "Working Committee on Medical Treatment" as the evaluation of existing forms of treatments and diagnosis was added to its duty.

A second federal level subcommittee, the "Valuation Committee", is responsible to set the number of points per kind of treatment in the Uniform Evaluation Standard (§ 87 SGB V). This committee, which is composed of sickness funds representatives and of physicians, discusses and determines the number of points for existing and for new medical procedures. If there is sufficiently high statistical evidence that the overall number of a certain treatment is extended (or diminished) without proper medical indication, a revaluation of the existing number of points may be initiated to set the right incentives to the physicians. The Valuation Committee has started to outline the reimbursable technology and its indications for use. However, up to now only a few treatments in the Uniform Evaluation Standard have precisely described indications. In addition, diverging financial incentives between physicians and health insurance funds as well as distribution conflicts between the various groups of medical specialists may distort an efficient allocation.

---

[38] Approval e.g. required a randomized controlled trial, a cohort study or the comparison of time series together with non-controlled clinical trials.

The Uniform Evaluation Standard generally contributes a higher number of points to groups of treatments which are more complex, whereas inexpensive and low-cost services get a lower score. Besides about 150 basic services like consultations, screening and visits, the physician services are systematized by characteristics. In addition, the Uniform Evaluation Standard lists some preconditions for reimbursement, e.g. particular indications for use or exclusions of other services during the same visit.[39]

As described above and as being shown in Table 2.2, each kind of technology is associated with a certain number of points. However, this number of points has to be connected with a price, the point value.

In the fee-for-service remuneration system there is a predetermined point value. Contrary, in a point system with a fixed total budget, at the end of an accounting period the overall budget is divided by the sum of the points collected by all physicians. Therefore the value of the point in this specific prospective payment system is determined ex post.

In the German outpatient market, at the end of a quarter each single physician bills the regional association of panel doctors the number of collected points for patients insured with a statutory health insurance fund and identifies the services according to the codes of the uniform evaluation standard. Prior to the residual payment of an accounting period the regional associations of panel doctors have to control, record and sum up the points and data that compose the basis of the reimbursement calculations. There are for the most part randomly taken control mechanism to uncover false claims e.g., faced on comparisons of utilization. In this case the very physician has to justify his submitted treatments to avoid financial penalties. Additional statutes of the regional associations of panel doctors can modify the reimbursement to some degree through the Remuneration Distribution

---

[39]Medical treatments for privately insured patients are remunerated by the practicing doctors' tariff schedule, called "Amtliche Gebührenordnung für Ärzte", "GO". Like the uniform evaluation standard this system also defines every single treatment in a scoring model.

Scale to adjust for unexpected variations between treatment characteristics and groups of physicians.

Table 2.2: Examples of services and the associated points attributed in the Uniform Evaluation Standard 1996

Service	Number of points
Basic fee per patient per 3 months	60 - 575 depending on speciality of physician and status of patient (working / retired)
Surcharge for regular care (per 3 months), Nephrologists for patients needing dialysis, Oncologists for patients with cancer or Rheumatologists for patients with patients with rheumatoid arthritis	900
Consultation fee (practice)	50
Diagnosis and/or therapy of psychiatric disorder through physician-patient conversation, duration at least 15 min.	450
Consultation fee (home visit)	400 (non urgent) 600 (urgen)
Antenatal care per 3 months	1850
Cancer screening	260 (men) 310 (women)
Health checkup	780
ECG	250
Osteodensitometry	450

Chapter 3

Remuneration of Physician Services: A Survey

3.1 The Economics of Physician Contracts

Although economists have devoted much time trying to understand the market of physician services especially in the U.S.A., this market remains relatively poorly understood.[40] Other markets like the German one for physician services even lack a rigorous analytical framework as well as empirical evidence for important questions concerning remuneration and information. This is amazing, because it is a sector of enormous economic relevance. This observation can be explained by several factors like information asymmetries, ex-post moral hazard and multiple agency that distinguish the market for physician services from other "textbook" markets, which make a thorough analysis relatively complicated.

Information asymmetries: The market for health services departs in several ways from the standard partial equilibrium model. In the standard model, consumers are sovereign and the volume and kinds of goods and services

---

[40]See also Gaynor (1994).

produced respond to independent consumer demands. In the market for health services, by contrast, consumers' demands are strongly influenced by information asymmetries in favor of health care providers In most cases it is difficult for a person who is sick or injured to accurately evaluate the cause and to determine the best treatment. Hence, patients have to rely on physicians (in ambulatory as well as in hospital care) to tell them what medical services they need.[41] Therefore it is difficult for patients to act as informed buyers.

Ex-Post Moral Hazard: One consequence of health insurance is ex-post moral hazard: insured patients demand more services than they would without insurance. By lowering the marginal cost of care to the individual, health insurance encourages the use of excessive health care services.[42]

Multiple Agency Relationships: In the market for physician services agency relationships between physician and patient, physician and insurance and patient and insurance exist. This thesis concentrates on the interrelations between physician and patient and physician and insurer and its focus is on patient sovereignty.[43]

Complex Price Systems: One of the implications of these multiple relationships are complex remuneration systems. In Germany they are the result of a negotiation process between physician and statutory funds. The remuneration of physicians acts - as any price - as an allocation and distribution mechanism by steering the factor input and the income of the physicians as well as the income distribution between physicians. In particular, the remuneration of physicians influences[44]

---

[41]Even ex post, patients often cannot determine the extent of the service that was required ex ante.

[42]For a detailed treatment of ex-post moral hazard in health care, see e.g. the seminal work of Pauly (1968).

[43]For a discussion of these factors see Arrow (1963), Zeckhauser (1970) and Dranove and White (1987).

[44]See also Thiemeyer (1985).

- the kind and amount of treatment including effort, costs and quality of the various treatments

- the distribution of the total expenditures on individual doctors' practices

- the relative distribution of treatments and income on different groups of physicians

- the decision to choose the profession of a physician and the decision to work in the market for physician services rather than in hospitals or in alternative markets like pharmacy or consulting.

Imperfect agency between the physician and the patient is the key element of the market for physician services and is at the core of one of the most debated topics in health care, the so-called "supplier induced demand". In the following Section 3.2 we first theoretically investigate this notion, before, in Section 3.3, we classify the empirical findings of various markets for physician services.

3.2 Theory of Supplier Induced Demand

In the literature the term "supplier induced demand" refers to the phenomenon of physicians deviating from their agency responsibilities to provide care for their self-interest. In other words, physicians are able to choose methods and intensity of treatments which a patient would not choose if he had the same information as the physician.

The notion that suppliers of medical care can create demand for their services dates back to Shain and Roemer (1959) and Roemer (1961), who found very strong correlations between the average availability of hospital beds per 1,000 population and rates of utilization as measured by hospital days per 1,000 population. This observation led to the slogan "a bed built is a bed filled" and became known as Roemer's Law.[45]

If health care providers can exert–due to information asymmetry–a direct influence on demand, the ways markets normally function are subverted. The effects of supplier induced demand are one of the major theoretical and political issues in health economics. A review of the theoretical literature is given by Feldman and Sloan (1988), Rice and Labelle (1989) and Labelle, Stoddart, and Rice (1994). The importance of this issue in the political debate is made clear by the following statement of Reinhardt (1989):

"The issue of physician-induced demand obviously goes straight to the heart of probably the major controversy in contemporary health policy, namely, the question whether adequate control over resource allocation to and within health care is best achieved through the demand side...or through regulatory controls on the supply side" (p. 339).

In this Section, the theoretical aspects of supplier induced demand that are important for a better understanding of the theoretical models in Chapter 4 are discussed. In modeling physician behavior it is generally assumed that the physician's utility depends positively on his income, leisure, and on delivery of the "appropriate" amount of care. This appropriate amount of care can enter utility directly, e.g. through "internal conscience" (e.g. Evans (1974), McGuire and Pauly (1992)) or by explicitly modeling the information asymmetries, where as a result of a reputation process excessively demand inducing physicians are punished through future reductions in true patient demand (Dranove (1988), Wolinsky (1993, 1995), Emons (1997)). As a result the physician faces a trade-off between an increase in current income and either a direct utility gain or an increase in discounted future income. In Subsection 3.2.1 it is shown that the reaction of the optimal level of inducement to changes in the number of physicians in the market is ambiguous in a fairly general model. However, in a model with more

---

[45]Other terms found in the literature are Say's Law and Roemer Effect for hospital beds or Parkinson's Law. See Feldman and Sloan (1988).

restrictions on preferences and the demand function it is possible to derive conditions for a positive effect of the availability of physicians on the degree of inducement. Subsection 3.2.2 presents a further strand of the inducement literature where the informational asymmetries between physicians and patients are modeled explicitly. It is shown and discussed how separation, monitoring, reputation and capacity limits can constrain supplier induced demand.

In Section 3.3 we provide an overview of the empirical studies on supplier induced demand.

3.2.1   Direct Inducement

The term "supplier induced demand" has been heavily debated as it questions whether the traditional relationship between demand and supply (the so-called neoclassical school) functions on the medical care market. Although an impressive range of papers on this subject has been published, the debate about improved availability vs. induced demand is not yet resolved.[46] As it will be discussed in more details in Subsection 3.2.1 and in Section 3.3, this is primarily due to the methodological limitation of the supplier induced demand literature to explain the availability effect. In particular "price-induced" and "supply-induced" increases in utilization have to be considered. This can be demonstrated by reference to Figure 3.1.

Figure 3.1 depicts the total demand D for and supply S of physician services in a given market area with corresponding prices P and quantities Q. It is assumed that total demand decreases as the price increases and that total supply increases as the price increases. Perfect competition leads to a market equilibrium price P_1 and an associated number of treatments Q_1. By illustrating the distinction between "price-inducement" and "supply-inducement" diagrammatically, it can be shown that outcomes from the

---

[46]Examples for recent papers focusing on this issue are Carlsen and Grytten (1998) and Dranove and Wehner (1994).

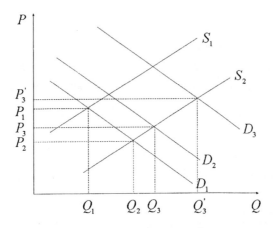

Figure 3.1: The consequences of increased supply: SID-effect and availability effect

market of physician services are consistent with the supplier induced models as well as neoclassical models.[47] An increase of physician supply will ceteris paribus shift the market supply from S_1 to S_2. Standard "neoclassical" analysis would predict that health care suppliers would cut prices from P_1 to P_2 and quantity demanded would increase from Q_1 to Q_2. Total spending would increase, decrease or stay the same, depending on the demand elasticity. Market entry also has an effect on the access costs of utilization as by e.g. falling waiting and travel time the patient's shadow price of utilization will fall and will shift market demand from D_1 to D_2 (standard "price-inducement"). Therefore prices will rise from P_2 to P_3 and quantity from Q_2 to Q_3.

In the "supplier-inducement" model a fall in price and a fall in physician's market share of patients and income due to market entry provides an incentive to physicians to use their discretionary influence to shift demand in order to maintain physicians' incomes. Physicians induce patients through

---

[47] For the discussion between the "neoclassical school" and the "supplier induced demand - school" see Reinhardt (1978, 1985).

subtle forms of "persuasion" to demand more treatments at any given price level. Therefore an increase in supply leads to an increase in demand through supplier induction, indicated by the additional shift from D_2 to D_3, which again pushes up prices and quantities to P'_3 and Q'_3 respectively.

This very simple comparative analysis of the range and implications of physician supply has shown that under the supplier induced demand approach as well as under the neoclassical approach an unambiguous positive effect on the number of treatments exist: For the positive effect on utilization the downward shift of the supply curve is sufficient. The new equilibrium price may be lower or even higher under either approach depending on the net effect of the downward shift in supply and the upward shift in demand. If the upward shift of demand under both approaches is significantly high, the equilibrium fee may rise above the initial level.

A Formal Analysis of Direct Inducement

The argument that physicians can induce demand to their advantage by exerting direct, non-price influence on the demand for their own services was first presented by Evans (1974). Evans discusses both the physician's professional (ethical) and economic behavior. In his approach Evans argues that the individual physician can shift out demand through inducing activities. However, as the analysis of Evans is more on a verbal basis and as the theoretical mechanism as well as the conclusions are not clear, we present a more rigorous framework to make the phenomenon of inducement more visible.

Starting our formal analysis, we investigate the demand for these kind of services first. As - analogue to Evans - the physician - e.g. as a monopolistic competitor[48] - has some market power, the individual doctor faces a demand function N falling in the price per treatment P, which can be written as

---

[48]The analysis is based on an individual physician as is common in this strand of literature and not on the interactions between physicians in the market.

follows:

$$N = F(P, D, R) \tag{3.1}$$

In addition to P the demand function is influenced by D. D is the physician's exerted discretionary influence to augment demand[49], hence $\frac{\partial F}{\partial D} > 0$. Finally, the demand function also depends on R, the ratio between population and physicians. The more physicians are in the market, c.p. the population share R will be diminished and therefore fewer patients show up by the physician. To simplify the analysis, we assume that demand spreads proportionally to the physicians in the market,[50] so that N is linearly homogeneous in R and therefore we can rewrite the demand function as:

$$N = R \cdot f(P, D); f(P, D) \equiv F(P, D, 1) \tag{3.2}$$

The physicians' profits, which are equal to the physicians' income, can be written as:

$$\Pi \equiv Y = P \cdot N - C(N) \tag{3.3}$$

Π is the profit with price P times the number of treatments N minus costs $C(N)$ as in a standard textbook monopoly:

$$\Pi = P \cdot R \cdot f(P, D) - C[R \cdot f(P, D)] \tag{3.4}$$

The physician is not a profit maximizer, but a utility maximizer: He gets positive utility out of income (profit), negative utility out of his workload (number of treatments performed), and also D, the "discretionary" factor

---

[49]See Evans (1974, p.166) .

[50]Like in a Salop Model or in a Hotelling model with market entry one can imagine that physicians are spread equally on a circle or a line. Therefore in a general approach this is a reasonably assumption to make. In practical terms an entering physician would e.g. choose a rural area with a small physician/population ratio instead of open up a doctor's practice in a quarter of a city with a very high ratio.

that the physician can persuade the patient to demand more treatments, enters utility negatively. This can be interpreted as a guilt feeling because of the attempt to convince the patients to demand treatments that are medically not indicated. This "discretion" also contradicts the oath of Hippokrates, where the physician acts - in contractual terms - as a perfect agent for the patient. In addition a physician may fear to lose his reputation, e. g. his "approbation", if sufficient control mechanisms are in place. Therefore the utility function can be written as follows:

$$U = U(Y, W, D) \qquad (3.5)$$

with $U_Y > 0$; $U_W < 0^{51}$ and $U_D < 0.^{52}$

Setting up the maximization problem of the individual physician leads to:

$$\max U(Y, W, D)$$
$$\text{s.t.} \quad (1) \quad Y = P \cdot R \cdot f - C(R \cdot f(P, D)) \qquad (3.6)$$
$$\text{s.t.} \quad (2) \quad W = N = R \cdot f(P, D)$$

The first constraint is simply the definition of income (profits)[53] and the second is the equilibrium condition that workload (treatments performed) equals the demanded treatments.

---

[51] In this approach, what we call "Evans-type model", workload (treatments performed) shows up in the definition of the utility function and in the cost function. Evan's inclusion of workload into the utility function would make sense, if Y were only revenue minus expenditure and if the physician does not pay himself calculated entrepreneurial wages, that is, Y is only revenue minus operating costs of the practice.

[52] Throughout this chapter, for clarity and simplicity, we shall adopt the convention of letting primes denote total derivatives and appropriate subscripts denote partial derivatives. Thus, we shall let $f'(X) \equiv \frac{df}{dX}$; $f_i(X_1, ..., X_n) \equiv \frac{\partial f}{\partial X_i}$; $f_{ij}(X_1, ..., X_n) \equiv \frac{\partial^2 f}{\partial X_i \partial X_j}$ etc.

[53] Evans (1974) does not give a precise definition of income. We argue that the only reasonable definition of the physician's income are the revenues minus the physician's practice costs.

Substituting (1) and (2) into the utility function, we get the following unconstrained maximization problem:

$$\max_{P,D} U = U[P \cdot R \cdot f(P,D) - C[R \cdot f(P,D)], R \cdot f(P,D), D] \qquad (3.7)$$

In equilibrium this utility maximization problem yields the following first-order conditions:

$$
\text{FOC for } \quad P: \quad \overbrace{U_Y}^{(+)} \underbrace{[P \cdot R \cdot f_P + R \cdot f -}_{\text{MR of a price change}} \underbrace{R \cdot C' \cdot f_P]}_{\text{MC of a price change}} +
$$

$$
\overbrace{U_W}^{(-)} \cdot \underbrace{R \cdot \overbrace{f_P}^{(-)}}_{\text{demand change (workload change) due to price change}} = 0 \qquad (3.8)
$$

$$
\text{FOC for } \quad D: \quad \overbrace{U_Y}^{(+)} \underbrace{[P \cdot R \cdot f_D - R \cdot C' \cdot f_D]}_{\text{Marginal Profits of a D-change}} + U_W \cdot R \cdot f_D + \overbrace{U_D}^{(-)} = 0
$$

$$(3.9)$$

Equation 3.8, the first order condition for P, shows that the marginal profits are negative in this optimum. The physician sets a price which is higher than in the standard monopoly case. In the normal monopoly case marginal revenues minus marginal costs and hence marginal profits are zero. In our case marginal profit is expressed in utility by multiplication with the term U_Y and there is an additional term: $U_W \cdot R \cdot f_P$. As demand is inverse to price as well as utility ($U_W < 0$) is inverse to workload (number of treatments performed), this additional term is positive. Since $U_Y > 0$, ($P \cdot R \cdot f_P + R \cdot f(P,D) - R \cdot C'f_P$) has to be negative at an optimum. If for example at the optimum the price increases by an infinitely small amount, demand and therefore the number of treatments performed will diminish. Hence utility will increase due to this reduced workload. On the other hand, the price increase leads to negative marginal profits, balancing out the positive effect through U_W. This is the reason for that at the optimum the physician chooses a price which is higher than the standard monopoly price.[54]

Equation 3.9, the first order condition for D, shows that the marginal gains through induced demand have to equal the marginal losses which come as associated costs of the physician's guilt feelings with this inducement.

Without the counterbalancing effect of the guilt feeling of inducement, the physician would induce demand infinitely or at least as far as possible. This can be seen as follows: In this case, $U_D = 0$, and equation 3.9 reads: $[U_Y[P \cdot R - R \cdot C'] + U_W \cdot R]f_D = 0$. So we have either $f_D = 0$, i.e. demand is induced as much as possible. Otherwise, demand is induced infinitely due to $[U_Y[P \cdot R - R \cdot C'] + U_W \cdot R]f_D > 0$.[55]

However, even as this model accounts for demand inducement and income endogenously, it fails to give definite predictions about the effects of increased physician availability on the level of D. Therefore with this "Evans-type model" we cannot say anything about comparative statics.[56]

One not very appealing feature of the above "Evans-type model" is that the workload (treatments performed) shows up in the definition of the utility function and in the cost function. We therefore modify the model such that C includes all opportunity costs of the physician.

Hence we propose the following set-up, which is a more tractable variant of the "Evans-type model": Now utility depends only on income Y (profits Π) and D (the "persuading-factor"), whereas the workload effects are included in the cost function.

---

[54]Recall, that the strategic variable in our model is price and not quantity.

[55]To proof this, equation 3.8 can be rewritten as $[U_Y[P \cdot R - R \cdot C'] + U_W \cdot R]f_P + U_Y \cdot R \cdot f(P, D) = 0$ (3.8a). With $f_P < 0$ and $U_Y \cdot R \cdot f(P, D) > 0$, $U_Y[P \cdot R - R \cdot C'] + U_W \cdot R > 0$.

[56]Ellis and McGuire (1986) note in a different model that depending on the utility function imperfect agency may also lead to an undersupply of care.

To simplify we use a quasi-linear utility function which has the following form:

$$U(Y, D) = Y - v(D) \tag{3.10}$$

v can have different forms: In the most general form v is convex and non-negative and $v = 0$, if $D = 0$. Therefore there does not exist a level of D, where the physician is "happy", but there exists a level of D, where the physician has a minimum of "not being happy". If $D > 0$, the physician feels uncomfortable as he has to persuade patients to consume more treatments than they would choose if they had the same information as the physician. This involves moral costs and therefore $v > 0$. In the opposite, when $D < 0$, the physician does not like to provide sufficient services to the patient which also comes with moral costs.[57]

Next, income (profits) is again given by:

$$Y \equiv \Pi = P \cdot N - C(N) \tag{3.11}$$

where N is demand, which is specified by $N = R \cdot f(P, D)$; $f_P < 0$ and $f_D > 0$.

It is quite reasonable to assume that the cost function is convex; that is $C' > 0$, $C'' > 0$. This might be because of monetary costs which are linear and because of additional effort costs which are convex.

Substituting N into Y and Y into U, we get the following unconstrained utility maximization problem:

$$\max_{P,D} \quad P \cdot R \cdot f(P, D) - C[R \cdot f(P, D)] - v(D) \tag{3.12}$$

---

[57]The properties of v can be formally expressed as follows: $v(D) \geq 0$, $v(0) = 0$

$$v'' > 0 \text{ and } \begin{cases} v' > 0 & \text{for} \quad D > 0 \\ v' < 0 & \text{for} \quad D < 0 \end{cases}$$

Now we can derive the first order conditions for P and D:

$$\text{FOC for } P: \quad \underbrace{R \cdot f + P \cdot R \cdot f_P}_{\text{MR of } \triangle \text{ P}} - \underbrace{C' \cdot R \cdot f_P}_{\text{MC of } \triangle P} = 0 \qquad (3.13)$$

$$\text{FOC for } D: \quad \underbrace{P \cdot R \cdot f_D - C' \cdot R \cdot f_D}_{\text{Marg. Profit of } \triangle \text{ D}} - \underbrace{v'}_{\text{MU of } \triangle \text{ D}} = 0 \qquad (3.14)$$

Equation 3.13, the first order condition for P, shows that as in the standard monopoly case the marginal revenues equal marginal costs in equilibrium and price is set above marginal costs.[58]

Equation 3.14, the first order condition for D, shows that a marginal change of the discretional inducement factor D leads to positive marginal profits, since $(P - C') > 0$. In an optimum, this positive effect is balanced by $v'(D)$, the marginal disutility of inducement, which can be interpreted as the marginal cost of D, expressed in utilities or in monetary terms. Increasing D rises demand and hence profits, which is always in the advantage of the physician. However, there are marginal moral costs of doing so. In the optimum, this marginal profits (marginal benefits) have to equal the marginal moral costs $v'(D)$. We show in the Appendix Section B.1 that D is always non-negatively chosen.

Investigating the market for physician services we are now able to turn to comparative statics. Imagine an exogenous shift in R, the ratio between population and physicians. With physicians entering the market, R will fall. To understand how price and the discretionary factor to induce demand will react to this change of the population/physician ratio we totally differentiate the FOC's (equation 3.13 and 3.14) and in addition we assume that the

---

[58]The FOC for P can be rewritten as $f + (P - C')f_P = 0$. Because $f(P, D) > 0$ and $f_P < 0$ from equation 3.13 it must be that $P - C' > 0$.

demand function is linear in P and D. Hence $f(P, D)$ becomes:

$$f(P, D) = \alpha - \beta P + \gamma D \qquad (3.15)$$

with α, β, $\gamma > 0$.

Doing comparative statics we get the following results, derived in the Appendix of Chapter B:

$$\frac{dD}{dR} = \frac{\beta\gamma[(P - C')(C''R\beta + 2) - C''Rf]}{\beta v''[RC''\beta + 2] - R\gamma^2} \qquad (3.16)$$

The denominator is assumed to be positive (to satisfy the second order conditions for a maximum); for a discussion see Appendix B.2. The numerator is negative if $(P - C')(C''R\beta + 2) - C''Rf < 0$, i. e.

$$\frac{(P - C')}{C''N} < \frac{1}{C''R\beta + 2} \qquad (3.17)$$

If the number of physicians increases, the population/physician ratio R decreases as some patients shift to the physicians which entered into the market. As the patients are now distributed to more physicians the - for the individual physician relevant - demand diminishes. Because of this reduced treatments performed and consequently reduced profits, the individual physician tries to compensate the lost demand by generating new demand, when patients are persuaded to accept more treatments. However, the sign $\frac{dD}{dR}$ is not unique; if inequality 3.17 holds, the above result is obtained.[59] Therefore it can not generally be concluded that more physicians in the outpatient market induce more demand each. It depends on the parameters of the very market, which appear in equation 3.17. If the mark-up is small, if costs are sufficiently convex and/or if demand is sufficiently big, more inducement is very probable.

Now we turn to the reaction of the price P, also derived in Appendix B.2:

---

[59]in addition to the assumption that a maximum exists, $\beta v''[RC''\beta + 2] - R\gamma^2 \equiv \Delta > 0$.

$$\frac{dP}{dR} = \frac{\overbrace{v''C''f\beta}^{(+)} + \overbrace{\gamma^2(1 + C''R\beta)}^{(+)}\overbrace{(P - C')}^{(+)} - \overbrace{C''\gamma^2 Rf}^{(+)}}{\beta v''[RC''\beta + 2] - R\gamma^2} \lessgtr 0 \qquad (3.18)$$

Investigating the numerator, it is not clear how an increase of physicians and therefore a reduction in R will influence the price P. On the one side, a decrease in R leads to a decrease in demand Rf, when the demand curve rotates inwards and leads to falling P. On the other hand, due to the discretional factor D, if a reduced R leads to higher (induced) demand, the demand curve shifts out. However, it is not clear which of these two demand effects with opposite directions is dominating the other one with respect to price. If γ is sufficiently small, i.e. demand cannot be very much influenced through the discretionary factor D, then the influence of the third term in the numerator is dominated by the first two terms and $\frac{dP}{dR} > 0$, i.e. more physicians lead to a lower price.

This result of the model with monopolistic competition is in line with Figure 3.1, which shows that price-effects are also not unique in a setting of perfect competition. There, only if increased demand through inducement is sufficiently large, the equilibrium price may rise above the initial price level as shown by the shift to D_3 in Figure 3.1. As it will be shown in the review-part of the empirical literature in Subsection 3.3.3, this identification problem due to price effects is still one of the major issues in health care economics.

The Target-Income Hypothesis of Supplier Induced Demand

In a second approach Evans also argues, that the physician is assumed to have rough targets for income and leisure and that the physician will adjust his behavior to achieve these targets. Under the target income hypothesis a falling exogenous population/physician ratio R leads to higher fees ($\frac{dP}{dR} > 0$)

in order to maintain income or utility instead of leading to lower fees and incomes. However, the target income hypothesis is unsatisfactory because it does not explain how the target income is established and why physicians do not consistently exploit their monopoly power by always pricing at profit-maximizing levels.[60]

Summary

In the "Evans-type model" physicians could induce demand directly by choosing the number of treatments via D. More physicians in the market reduce the population/physician ratio R and it is very plausible that this in turn leads the physician to induce demand (by an increase of the discretionary factor D). However, there are limitations on supplier induced demand, because the degree of inducement enters the physician's utility negatively or because physicians have an exogenous target income.

Another strand of literature models informational asymmetries between physicians and patients explicitly and therefore provides theoretical grounds for alternative explanations for why and under which conditions supplier induced demand is constrained.

3.2.2   Credence Goods

The theoretical literature about the informational aspects in the market for medical services goes back to Arrow (1963). The seminal article about fraudulent experts due to the informational asymmetry between physician and patient is the work of Darby and Karni (1973), who term such goods "credence goods". With a credence good, consumers (patients) cannot determine the extent of the service (treatment) that was needed. This information asymmetry between buyers (patients) and sellers (physicians)

---

[60]See Rice and Labelle (1989) for a review of the target-income literature and its applications to fee controls.

creates obvious incentives by the sellers (physicians) to cheat on the services. Darby and Karni discuss how reputation combined with market conditions affects the amount of fraud in such a market. However, their analysis does not contain a formal equilibrium concept.

The size of the formal literature on credence goods is still very small. Pitchik and Schotter (1987) describe a mixed-strategy equilibrium in an expert-customer game. In this model in equilibrium the experts randomize between either reporting truthfully or not, whereas customers randomize between acceptance and rejection of recommended treatments. Wolinsky (1993) investigates customer search for multiple opinions and reputation considerations. One possible equilibrium is that, where some experts (physicians) exclusively provide minor treatments while other experts engage in minor and major treatments. Consumers first visit a "minor-treatment" expert. When major treatment is recommended by this expert, the patient goes to a specialist for the actual treatment. Emons (1997) investigates economies of scope between diagnosis and repair (treatment), which can make the customer's consulting of several experts unattractive. In contrast to Wolinsky, Emons analyzes experts who are capacity constrained. An expert's incentives for fraudulent behavior therefore depends on the interplay of diagnosis and treatment prices, capacity and the number of clientele.

We present the model of Wolinsky (1993) in more detail, as this article nicely works out the relationships of the patients' search for multiple opinions and reputation considerations to reduce supplier induced demand. In addition this analysis was the first one which delivered a rigorous model of the agency relationship between physician and patient.

In this model of credence goods, applied to the market of physician services, the patient observes a symptom, but he does not know the nature and therefore the kind of treatment needed to cure his symptom. Consumers do not observe which treatment they obtain, only the outcome of the treatment i.e., whether their symptom is cured or not. There exists a probability w, which is common knowledge, that the health problem is a serious one (H-Problem) with high treatment costs and a probability $(1-w)$, that the health problem is a minor one with low costs, called L-Problem. By diagnosing the patient the physician finds out whether the patient is confronted with the serious health problem or with the minor one. Because of this agency relationship between physician and patient the physician has the incentive to misrepresent a minor treatment as a major one. Payment can only be conditioned on the outcome but not on the type of treatment, but consumers can search for the optimal treatment by demanding multiple diagnosis. However, these diagnoses are costly and therefore the patient faces search-costs of k per expert, independent of whether he is treated or not. This patient's search costs k should be interpreted as search-cum-diagnostic costs. The individual physician faces monetary costs $c_L = L$ and $c_H = H$ with $H > L$.

Following Wolinsky (1993), the structure of the game is the following:

- **Stage 0:** Nature chooses the type of the patient's symptom, the H-Problem with a priori probability w and the L-Problem with a priori probability $(1 - w)$.

- **Stage 1:** The physicians in the market simultaneously decide about

  - the individual price-vector (P_L, P_H), with $P_L \geq L$ and $P_H \geq H$.[61] If $P_H = \infty$, then physicians do not offer this treatment

  - the policy of recommendation, described by the probability $x \in [0, 1]$. With probability x the physician recommends the H-treatment, although the L-treatment would be sufficient.

- **Stage 2:** The patients observe the vector (P_L, P_H) and their own search experience, but they do not observe the physicians' recommendation policy. The patient chooses

---

[61]This assumes that a physician would not treat a patient at a price below costs.

- the physician

- a search plan of visiting physicians. In other words, each patient decides with what probability he will switch the physician. Given the strategy-space y_1, $y_2...y_\infty$, the patient will switch with the probability $1 - y_1$, with $y_1 \in [0,1]$, if the first physician has diagnosed an H-Treatment, with the probability $1 - y_2$ with $y_2 \in [0,1]$, if the second physician has diagnosed an H-Treatment etc. This means that the patient will continue to search, if he does not accept the recommended treatment

The individual physician's utility therefore can be expressed as follows:

$$U^{phy} = N_L(P_L - L) + N_H(P_H - H) \tag{3.19}$$

with N_i accounting for the number of patients, treated by the diagnosis $i = L$ and diagnosis $i = H$.

The utility of a patient who visits n physicians is described as follows:

$$U^{patient} = \begin{cases} B - P - nk & \text{if he is treated} \\ -nk & \text{if he is not treated} \end{cases} \tag{3.20}$$

with B being the benefit of a treatment to the patient.

This value B is assumed to be sufficiently large (above $H + k$) to assure that participation is always desirable for the patient.

To solve the game the concept of Perfect Bayesian Nash Equilibrium is used. There are multiple equilibria in this model:

Equilibrium with Fraud

In this equilibrium with fraud, all physicians announce the price vector $(P_L, P_H) = (L + e, H)$ and utilize the recommendation policy $0 < x < 1$ with e being a markup. Patients choose $0 < y_1 < 1$, $y_2, y_3, ...y_\infty = 0$. This means that the patients reject an H-recommendation with probability $1 - y_1$ when they come from the first consulted physician but accept any further treatment with certainty by the next physician. In this game physicians do not know if they are the one being consulted first or if they are number two in the row of visits by an individual patient.

The probabilities x and y and the markup e are chosen such that diagnosing a L-type, the physician must be indifferent between reporting truthfully and treating the minor illness which gives a profit of e, or claiming that it is a major illness, which brings the risk of loosing the customer.

Formally, this requires that

$$e = (H - L)\frac{y_1}{1 + x(1 - y_1)} + \frac{x(1 - y_1)}{1 + x(1 - y_1)} \qquad (3.21)$$

where $\frac{y_1}{1+x(1-y_1)}$ is the fraction of patients who are visiting the physician for the first time and who accept the major treatment with probability y_1 and $\frac{x(1-y_1)}{1+x(1-y_1)}$ is the fraction of patients who have visited another expert before and who will accept the major treatment with probability 1.

On the other hand, a patient being given the H-diagnosis must be indifferent between obtaining the treatment or going to another physician and obtaining treatment there. Therefore:

$$H = k + \frac{(1 - w)x}{w + (1 - w)x}((1 - x)(L + e) + x \cdot H) + \frac{w}{w + (1 - w)x}H \qquad (3.22)$$

where $\frac{(1-w)x}{w+(1-w)x}$ is the actualized, conditional probability of the patient having a L-type problem.[62] The equilibrium outcome incorporates a certain amount of fraud which balances the incentive to cheat (induce demand) and the incentive to search for another physician. The degree of fraud is just enough for the patient to seek second opinions, which in turn hinders physicians from always recommending the major treatment. To get this balance, the equilibrium price of the minor treatment has to embody a sufficient markup. The competition drives the price of the major treatment to its marginal costs and the equilibrium price for the H-treatment will be H.

We have not checked for out-of-equilibrium pricing strategies, but one can find appropriate beliefs such that this is indeed an equilibrium (for details Wolinsky 1993, 1995).

However, this equilibrium is not stable if a reasonable belief refinement is used. Assume that a physician does not announce the price vector $(P_L, P_H) = (L+e, H)$, but instead deviates to a specialization offer $(P_L, P_H) = (L+e, \infty)$, then a reasonable belief with regard to x would be $x = 0$. Under these beliefs patients on their first visit would choose this expert and the upper equilibrium with fraud would not exist.

Equilibria without Fraud

Depending on the size of the switching costs k two further types of equilibria exist:

1. If search costs $k > \frac{(1-w)(H-L)}{w}$, a market equilibrium (which minimizes patients' expected costs) exists, where all physicians offer $(P_L, P_H) = (H, H)$, patients just go to one physician and accept the treatment.

---

[62]This conditional probability follows because:

$$\text{Prob(L/Diagnosis H)} = \frac{\text{prob}(L \wedge \text{Diagnosis H})}{\text{prob(Diagnosis H)}} = \frac{(1-w)x}{w+(1-w)x}$$

2. "Separation equilibrium": If search costs $k < \frac{(1-w)(H-L)}{w}$, the market equilibrium that minimizes the patients' expected costs is, that some physicians employ the strategy (L, ∞) with $x = 0$, while others employ the strategy (H, H) with $x = 1$. Here, patients first visit a physician who offers (L, ∞) and, if he recommends the H-treatment, go to a physician who offers (H, H).

The dependency of the structure of the equilibrium on the size of the search costs k can be seen as follows:

The expected costs to the patient in the equilibrium, where patients first visit a "minor-treatment expert" and, if the H-treatment is recommended, switch to a "major-treatment expert" are $k + (1 - w)L + w(k + H)$, while the expected costs where all physicians offer the schedule (H, H) are $k + H$. These expected costs are the same for $k = (1 - w)\frac{(H-L)}{w}$. Hence, for low search costs the patient would prefer the specialization equilibrium, while for larger search costs he prefers to be treated by the first physician.[63]

Let us consider the "specialization" equilibrium in some more detail.

Why does a physician not deviate and offer a price vector $(L + \epsilon, H)$, for example? If a patient choosing this physician were to accept any recommended treatment, the physician would always recommend a H-diagnosis. But then the patient is better off by visiting a minor-treatment physician first. If however a patient choosing this physician were to reject a H-diagnosis with some probability, he must be indifferent between being treated for price H, or leaving the physician and going to a minor-treatment physician next. But this can never be better than going immediately to the minor treatment physician.

As markets for minor and major treatments act independently, competition drives the prices of both types of treatments to their respective costs. The

---

[63] For the proof, that this market equilibrium minimizes the expected costs of the patients, see Wolinsky (1993), p. 385.

physicians' incentive for fraudulent behavior is removed because physicians specialized in minor treatments lose their business when they recommend a major treatment.

Whether the market equilibrium is of the "specialization" type or not depends on three sizes. "Specialization" will be more probable,

1. the smaller the search costs k are,

2. the higher the difference between H and L is, in other words, the higher the incentive is to cheat,

3. the smaller w is, the probability of having to undergo major treatment, which decreases the ex-ante probability for having to go to a major-treatment expert.

This "specialization" scenario describes a feature we observe in the physician market: the separation between general practitioners and specialists. In the literature there are further possible solutions to the information problem in this credence good market to which we will turn now.

Monitoring

This can be done by a second diagnosis. If diagnosis by independent experts are different, the deviating physician will be faced with hard punishment. This will temper the incentive for physicians to increase the volume of treatment. Control mechanism to uncover false claims can also be taken randomly.

Reputation

To demonstrate how reputation can prevent fraudulent behavior, we again refer to Wolinksy (1993). The previous model is slightly altered: Now physicians do not commit to the cost of treatment in advance. The patients confer their health problem to a physician who first makes the treatment and then bills the patient. Patients experience two independent health problems and hence show up by a physician for two periods. In the beginning of each period the physicians announce their price schedule. Then each customer chooses a physician to whom he entrusts his problem. After the treatment the physician can claim the treatment was H or L and accordingly charge the price he has announced for that treatment. It is assumed that a physician cannot tell whether a patient is in his first or in his second visit.

Therefore $x \in [0,1]$ must be reinterpreted as the probability with which patients with the minor problem will be charged for the major problem.

There exist two symmetric equilibria:

1. Equilibrium, where $L < P_L = P_H < H$. Here the patients stay with their physician, independent of the treatment. This equilibrium minimizes patients' expected costs.

2. Equilibrium, where $P_L > L$, $P_H = H$ and where $x = 0$. Here, the patients switch the physician in the second period, if they had been treated for an H-problem in the first period.

In both equilibria the incentive for physicians to be correct lies in the prospect of repeat business. In the first equilibrium this outlook offsets the physician's incentive to reject an H-type patient.[64] Although physicians treat this kind of patients at a price below costs, they compensate this loss with minor treatments.

In the second equilibrium the prospect of a further treatment offsets the physicians' incentive to charge a patient for a major health problem and to gain $P_H - P_L$, when the problem is a minor one.

---

[64] In this reputation model the physician is allowed to reject a patient. We do not discuss this issue here. See Wolinsky (1993) for details.

Capacity (Emons, 1997)

Emons consider physicians who are capacity constrained. If too many patients turn up, a physician may have to ration the treatment for his patients. Otherwise he may be faced by idle capacity. In Emon's model treatment is possible only after diagnosis and physicians charge separate prices for diagnosis and treatment. Analyzing the interaction of prices, capacity and the number of patients the following results are derived: If physicians work at full capacity and if the profit per treatment and the profit per diagnosis is the same (Emons calls this equal compensation prices), the physicians will be able to diagnose in an honest manner as they are indifferent between diagnosis and treatment. As demand exceeds the physicians' capacity, physicians charge those equal compensation prices which make consumers indifferent between buying and not-buying the physician services. Thus, given these reservation prices, physicians are honest and grasp the entire surplus.

If the physicians do not have enough patients they might have the incentive to overtreat to get some money out of the otherwise idle capacity. However, the physician's incentive to treat too much vanishes if there is no money in treatment: With idle capacity Bertrand competition drives prices down to marginal costs. Since at these marginal cost prices diagnosis as well as treatment leads to zero profits, physicians behave honestly. In this case the patients confiscate the entire surplus.

Application of Credence Goods Models to the German Market for Physician Services[65]

Applying the described possible solutions (equilibria) to the German market for physician services, the following brief observations can be made:

---

[65]Although insurance in the German health care sector is important the basic idea of these models still applies, when there are non-monetary costs to the patients of low and high treatments.

- Separation: In the German market for physician services there is some separation of major and minor treatments. Separation in this market occurs in the sense that there are generalists and specialists. For example, patients typically see a general practitioner or internist for diagnosis first and are then referred to a specialist. Also, we observe separation between physicians, who recommend medicine, and pharmacists, who sell the medicine.

- Monitoring: In Germany the regional physician associations are not only responsible for paying the physicians in outpatient care, but also for monitoring them and tempering the tendency for physicians to increase treatment volume. The associations financially penalize physicians with service volumes well beyond the average if this cannot be explained by case mix. Although there are some obscure cases which make it into the public press, supplier induced demand is probably detected in rare cases: Administrative costs for monitoring detailed service items are high and treatment standards not well developed. In addition, the association for contract doctors represents the interests of the physicians versus the statutory health insurers and the government by bargaining about the amount of the global budget, which might reduce its incentive to monitor its member physicians.

- Reputation: As the patients in most cases[66] do not have to pay a price for the visit to the physician[67] a reputation equilbrium might be impossible if over-treatment does not incorporate non-monetary costs. If patients are indifferent between different forms of treatments, physicians will always choose the major treatment. This behavior exerts an externality through the insurance system in the form of higher contribution rates. If, on the other hand, the major treatment causes additional non-monetary costs, like inconveniences of medical

---

[66]For a discussion see e.g. Süddeutsche Zeitung (2000).

[67]Since 1989 there is some copayment to the medication which a physician prescribes, however the visit to the physician is free due to insurance.

care, then reputation can still be important in a market with health insurance.

- Capacity: There was considerable growth in the number of physicians and also in the number of physicians per capita prior to 1990. Figure 3.2 illustrates the trend for physicians in the German market for physician services and as a whole in Germany. Although demand was likely to grow over this period due to the aging of the population and the rising number of the treatment-catalogue based on technological progress, this considerable growth in the number of physicians per capita could have strengthened supplier-induced demand. As the prices per treatment are set by the governing body and not by the physicians, there is no competitive pressure to assure equal compensation prices.

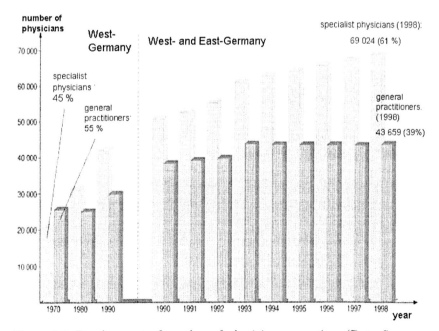

Figure 3.2: Development of number of physicians over time (Data Source: Federal Association of Panel Doctors

A further strand of literature still in its infancy attempts to combine the agency relationships between physicians and patients and patients and insurers, i.e. see Ellis and McGuire (1990) and Ma and McGuire (1997). As this thesis does not focus on ex-post moral hazard, we do not discuss this topic here.

3.3   Empirical Evidence for Supplier Induced Demand

In this section we investigate the empirical evidence for supplier induced demand in the market for physician services. The numerous articles in this field can be categorized into three broad strands.

The first strand analyzes the relationship between physicians per capita of population and the price or the number of treatments. In the simplest case the idea is as follows. If there is no inducement then the number of treatments should be only a function of actual illnesses and therefore independent of the number of physicians. However, if each physician induces to a certain extent, then total inducement and therefore the total number of treatments is a function of the number of physicians in a certain region. Unfortunately, reality is not quite that simple and many tests of this hypotheses face a number of econometric problems.

The second strand concentrates on the influence of exogenous changes in physician financing on the behaviour of physicians. Most of the articles in this area estimate the response of the number of treatments to exogenous fee reductions. Generally these studies do find evidence of a quantity reaction, however, the interpretation of these findings is difficult. The alternative to the inducement hypothesis is a supply response of physicians. Only one study successfully avoids this problem by concentrating on a special case of qualitative reaction and thereby provides more convincing evidence for inducement.

The third strand searches directly for evidence of supplier induced demand. This type of study looks mainly on the differential probability of treatment for well informed and less well informed patients. A straightforward example for well informed patients are physicians and their families. The results show that for certain treatments, like gall bladder operations, there is a high probability of inducement. However, not all studies confirm SID.

3.3.1 Physician Density and Number or Price of Treatments

As most of the original studies use cross-sectional data to examine the relationship between the number of physicians per capita and price or utilization across areas, this strand of empirical literature is surveyed and discussed first.

As already mentioned, the estimation of SID effects is not straightforward. To achieve a better understanding of the issues involved, it is instructive to demonstrate the econometric problems by a simple algebraic example. Consider the following linear demand-supply model model for a certain area:

$$N_D = a_0 + a_1 P + a_2 Y + a_3 A + u_1$$
$$N_S = b_0 + b_1 P + b_2 X + b_3 A + u_2$$

$$(3.23)$$

where N_D and N_S represent demand for and supply of physician services in this area and P represents the price. In the demand equation exogenous variables like income and education are expressed by the term Y, whereas in the supply function exogenous variables as input prices are represented by X. The availability of physicians is expressed by variable A.[68]

---

[68] Alternatively, P can be interpreted as an access price, for example the time price of visiting a physician. In this case, the second equation has a different meaning, however. It is now a price equation, where the access price is a function of the number of treatments, availability and other variables. Implicitly, this reformulation of the model assumes that physicians meet any demand. No rationing occurs. However, physicians impose increasing costs on patients when the number of treatments goes up.

Supplier induced demand in this model takes the form $a_3 > 0$ (see Fuchs 1978). If each physician induces a certain amount of demand, aggregate demand in a region is an increasing function of the availability of physicians in this area. In equilibrium supply equals demand $N = N_D = N_S$ and it is possible to derive the following reduced form of the model:

$$N = c_0 + c_1 X + c_2 Y + c_3 A + v \qquad (3.24)$$

with

$$c_3 = \frac{a_3 - \frac{b_3 a_1}{b_1}}{1 - \frac{a_1}{b_1}} \qquad (3.25)$$

It is important to note that supplier induced demand is not a necessary condition for a positive conditional correlation between the quantity of treatments in equilibrium and the availability of physicians ($c_3 > 0$). If availability increases supply ($b_3 > 0$) and demand is price sensitive ($a_1 < 0$) then the correlation will be positive even if $a_3 = 0$. In some cases there exists a priori information that a_1 is very low, but this is the exception rather than the rule.

It is therefore necessary to identify the demand equation and thereby a_3 to clarify the importance of supplier induced demand. Identification requires the existence of an instrumental variable that can be used to instrument the price P in the demand equation. A valid instrument in this application is a variable in X that is influencing supply but not demand, i.e. it is not a member of Y, and is exogenous. Unfortunately, as discussed below, the validity of suggested instruments is often in doubt.

Even if a proper instrument were available, many authors argue that this would still not be sufficient because of a second identification problem due to the endogeneity of A. This is discussed for example in Auster and Oaxaca (1981), Phelps (1986), and Feldman and Sloan (1989). More specifically, it is argued that A is a function of demand:[69]

$$A = d_0 + d_1 N_D + d_2 Z + u_3 \qquad (3.26)$$

If this is true we not only need instruments for P, but we also need instruments for A in the demand equation, because A is correlated with the error term u_1. An instrument would be given by an exogenous variable Z, influencing availability, that is different from the variables in Y and the instrument used for P. The following discussion of empirical work in this area shows that these requirements for econometric identification are difficult to fulfill. Hence, the actual amount of supplier induced demand remains a heavily debated topic in applied research.

The studies on SID generally analyze a specific treatment. For example, Fuchs (1978) and Cromwell and Mitchell (1988) estimate the response of the utilization of surgery to an increased supply of surgeons across areas. Both papers find strong evidence for demand inducement by investigating a cross-section of locations over several years. Fuchs argues that the first identification problem is not important here, because of a very low price elasticity of surgery demand ($a_1 \approx 0$). Fuchs as well as Cromwell and Mitchell try to overcome the second identification problem using instruments such as a dummy for nonmetropolitan-like regions, the number of colleges, per capita receipts of hotels, the proportion of the population that is white, climate and cultural opportunities. However, it is not clear, whether these variables are really uncorrelated with the disposition for surgery and therefore surgery demand. If not, then their suggested Z is an element of Y in the model and does not qualify as instrument.

This question is analyzed in more detail by Dranove and Wehner (1994). They show that standard estimation methods can lead to empirical results which are consistent with the inducement hypothesis where inducement is

---

[69]A similar argument can be made for the observed correlation between A and P, see Satterthwaite (1982).

impossible. They examine the number of childbirths and show that by using
the instrumental variables approach "evidence" of inducement for childbirth
can be found although physicians would have extreme difficulties doing this.
As a consequence, they argue that this popular technique to test supplier
induced demand with cross-section data on physician supply and utilization
fails to deal properly with the identification problem. They explain their
result by the low quality of the available instruments, which are shown to be
correlated with the error term in the demand equation.

A possible solution is to concentrate on special cases, where both identification problems are likely to be very small. Birch (1988) argues that in U.K.
dentistry a money price effect doesn't exist because of fixed fees for dental
care. Moreover, he uses the content of each visit as dependent variable to
exclude possible supply effects through reduced access costs. If the average
content of a visit in a region is not influencing the supply decision of dentists,
e.g. because it is unobservable, this is a promising approach. Both studies
along these lines, Birch (1988) and Grytten, Holst, and Laake (1990), find
significant inducement effects. Patients in districts with a high dentists-
population ratio receive considerably more services per treatment course
on average than patients in districts with fewer dentists. Birch's findings
imply that a 10 percent increase increase in dentist supply would increase
the average cost per treatment course by 2.5 percent. This result cannot be
explained by the greater dental care needs of the patient population since
the effect of dental health status has been covered by the inclusion of other
independent variables.

Rossiter and Wilensky (1983) explore the inducement hypothesis using data
from the 1977 US National Medical Care Expenditure Survey. They argue
that identification problems can be avoided using micro data on physician
initiated visits. In contrast to initial visits access prices are unlikely to
play a role here. Furthermore, the locational decision of physicians is
possibly not affected by this variable. They test supplier induced demand
by estimating the effect of the availability of physicians on the likelihood

of physician-initiated visits, total physician-initiated expenditures etc. The authors' findings are ambiguous. The estimated elasticity of the likelihood of physician-initiated visits with respect to availability is 0.125 and statistically significant. Total physician-initiated expenditures on the other hand are not affected by the population/physician ratio.

Using a similar approach, Tussing (1983) and Tussing and Wojtowycz (1986) find stronger evidence for supplier induced demand by examining health care in Ireland. In a study of Medicare beneficiaries, by contrast, Escarce (1992) concludes that an increased number of surgeons in the market increased the initial number of contacts with surgeons but had only a small effect on the treatment intensity of subsequent visits. Similarly, Grytten, Carlsen, and Sorensen (1995) in an investigation of the Norwegian market for physician services do not find inducement with respect to physician-initiated visits, only for the provision of laboratory tests.

3.3.2 Exogenous Income Shocks and Physician Behaviour

The second strand in the literature examines the impact of exogenous shocks to physician income, like fee reductions or changes in demand, on the behaviour of physicians. Unfortunately, economic theory does not always make clear predictions on the expected direction of the effect. For example, some argue that a decrease in fees followed by an increase in the quantity of services supports the supplier induced demand hypotheses because physicians are trying to maintain their level of income. Others argue that an increase in physicians' services following an increase in fees is evidence of supplier induced demand because physicians now make more money per treatment and therefore raise the number of treatments.

Examples of this strand of literature with exogenous income shocks are Holahan and Scanlon (1978), Rice (1983), Barer, Labelle, Morris, Evans, and

Stoddart (1978), Mitchell and Rosenbach (1989), Hurley, Labelle, and Rice (1990) and Krasnik, Groenewegen, Pedersen, Scholten, Mooney, Gottschau, Flierman, and Damsgaard (1990). Holahan and Scanlon (1978) and Mitchell and Rosenbach (1989) both examine the effect of fee controls that were implemented to constrain the rate of growth in fees in the U.S. Medicare program. Holahan and Scanlon find that quantity and intensity of services provided to Medicare beneficiaries increased up to 10 per cent per year (total physicians' revenues increased by 10-13 percent per year) during the Nixon Administration's Economic Stabilization Program, which lasted from 1971 to 1974. They also find that in 1975, when this program was lifted, the quantity of services provided leveled off and actually declined 9 percent for general practitioners, while physicians raised their prices by 23 percent on average. Mitchell and Rosenbach (1989) estimated that during the Medicare fee freeze from 1984 to 1986 expenditures per beneficiary increased by 29.5 percent, resulting from an increasing number of treatments and complexity of services.

Rice (1983) examines an exogenous change in Medicare prices in Colorado and claims that his results show that physicians induce extra demand when fees are reduced. He finds that a 10 percent decline in physician reimbursement led to a 6.1 percent increase in intensity of medical services and a 2.7 percent intensity of surgical services. Barer, Labelle, Morris, Evans, and Stoddart (1978) find that the number of treatments did not respond to a fee cut in British Columbia. Hurley, Labelle, and Rice (1990) explore the impact of fee changes on utilization for a set of 28 procedures billed by physicians in Ontario, Canada under the Health Insurance Plan. Their findings indicate that there is no general response of utilization to fee changes.

It should be noted, that reactions to fee changes can also be explained by the market mechanism. If there is a price ceiling, the quantity response depends on the shape of the supply curve. If, for example, the fixed price is raised exogenously by the government, an upward (downward) sloping supply function implies an increase (decrease) in the number of treatments performed. This argument assumes that the price ceiling did lead to rationing of demand. Morevover, the individual labour supply of physicians or the supply of new physicians has to be sufficiently elastic to explain the quantitative results. While this is questionable it is nonetheless an important caveat against the usual interpretation of the results.

A more recent article by Gruber and Owings (1996) avoids most of these problems. They focus on the effect of changes in fertility rates on obstetricians' use of cesarean section in deliveries. A decline in the fertility rate represents a shock that shifts the demand for obstetric services inwards and should reduce the incomes of obstetricians. The observed decline in fertility in the United States in the period between 1970 and 1982 by 13.5 percent is a good example. Changes in fertility have the advantage of being truly exogenous events. An important possibility for obstetricians to react is their decision on the form of delivery, because cesarean sections are commonly agreed to be more profitable than vaginal deliveries.[70]

In a theoretical model Gruber and Owings show that the reaction of physicians to a negative shock in fertility rates is an unambiguous increase in inducement, i.e. an increase in the share of cesarean section in all deliveries. In their empirical estimates they find a strong correlation between within state increases in cesarean rates and within state declines in fertility. These authors therefore argue that the income pressure on obstetrician/gynecologists due to the declining fertility led them to substitute from normal childbirth toward the higher reimbursed cesarean delivery. Being carried out in only 5 percent in 1970, cesarean delivery had risen by over 240 percent in the subsequent 12 years. Because inducement is not measured as a quantity variable, but rather as a certain quality of treatment the study is free from the identification problem from which the studies using fee cuts suffer. It therefore can be seen as convincing evidence in favor of the inducement hypothesis.

---

[70]For instance in Germany even for calculated 'per case' flat rates the remuneration for cesarean sections will be nearly twice as much as for vaginal deliveries, see Die Zeit (2000).

Another investigation, which is related to the third strand of the empirical literature, where opportunistic behavior of physicians is directly investigated, is the work done by Hickson, Altmeier, and Perrin (1987). This paper examines the response of physicians to price changes. The authors construct an experiment: 18 pediatric resident physicians in a clinic were selected randomly in two groups of 9 each. One group was assigned to be paid a fixed salary basis, the other to be paid on a fee-for-service reimbursement system. Patients were randomized among these physicians. The fee-for-service physicians scheduled more visits of patients, exceeded guidelines for pediatric care, but provided better continuity of care and were the reason for fewer visits to the emergency room. The salaried physicians were in less conformity with the guidelines of the American Academy of Pediatrics than their fee-for-service colleagues. One could conclude that fee-for-service remuneration leads to inducement while fixed salary involves shirking. However, the effect on total cost was ambiguous as physicians with the fee-for-service remuneration incorporated increased costs due to more treatment but reduced costs due to the reduced utilization of emergency room care.

The main inconvenience with the first two strands of literature is that they conduct an indirect search for supplier induced demand. In most cases data is on the market level rather than on individual physician level. For instance, studies of the first strand of literature examine the relationship between utilization and supply of medical care. As pure inducement is difficult to identify in such a setting, this kind of studies are in many cases not convincing. The next section summarizes the results of more direct approaches to the problem.

3.3.3 Direct Search for Supplier Induced Demand

The third strand of literature, the direct search for evidence of supplier induced demand, tries to explicitly explore individual decisions of patients and physicians to find evidence of opportunistic behavior. One possibility to circumvent the identification problem described above is to consider the choices of well-informed consumers and compare them with those of less informed consumers. The basic idea is that supplier induced demand can only occur if consumers are not well-informed. Hay and Leahy (1982) compared the quantity of care received by doctors and their families with that received by the rest of the population, controlling for other relevant factors. Presumably physicians and their families are well informed, and opportunism is more difficult with them. Interestingly, Hay and Leahy found that doctors and their families received more care than others, rather than less.

However, there is evidence about treatments for less informed patients without proper medical justification: One example is an investigation made by Domenighetti, Casabiaca, Gutzwiller, and Martinolli (1993) in the Swiss canton of Ticino. Of the seven most important operations the population average had about 33 percent more operation than physicians and their family members. In addition this comparative study found that lawyers and their families have about the same operation frequency as physicians and their relatives.

Another interesting example of this sort are the operations of gall bladders in the German health care market. Between 1990 and 1996 their number had risen by 150 percent through the introduction of outpatient endoscopic operation techniques. However, for the same indication, physicians show a rate of operation which is 84% lower than the rate of the average population.[71]

---

[71]Speech of the state secretary Christa Nickels at the health care congress on May, 11, 1999 in Heidelberg/Germany.

Related work was done by Kenkel (1990), where health information is investigated by survey responses about the interpretation of symptoms. Kenkel shows that more information increases the probability that a patient uses medical care. A possible explanation is that poorly informed patients underestimate the productivity of medical care. The test of inducement is based on theoretical results derived by Dranove (1988). Dranove shows that physicians will induce more demand with poorly informed patients. This hypothesis is not confirmed by the data. It turns out that conditional on the use of medical care less information has only an insignificant effect on the quantity demanded.

3.4   Conclusion

The discussion about imperfect agency in the market for physician services has been addressed by distinct theoretical models as well as by various empirical studies. The criticisms laid out above can be summarized as follows:[72]

- Lack of a rigorous theoretical model:

  It has been argued that many of the outcomes which have been observed in supplier induced demand studies are consistent with the predictions of both neoclassical and inducement models, and hence are ambivalent.[73] Further, many models have been criticized for

---

[72] For more details on the discussion issues i.e. see Reinhardt (1985), Ramsey and Wasow (1986), McGuire and Pauly (1992) and Labelle, Stoddart, and Rice (1994).

[73] In the theoretical literature of supplier induced demand there is an ongoing debate between the neoclassical school and the advocates of the inducement models. As Reinhardt (1985) describes: "The neoclassical prediction does have the virtue of emerging from a rigorous analytical structure. Its critics, however argue that this analytical structure rests on an overly narrow conception of human behaviour...(154)". The supporters of the inducement theory claim to derive their economic intuition primarily from first-hand experience by carefully observing the health-care sector. Their critics, in turn, argue that the target income thesis lacks a rigorous analytic underpinning. For this discussion see Reinhardt (1985) and Labelle, Stoddart, and Rice (1994).

serious conceptual shortcomings. For instance, as it is discussed in chapter 3.3., the major shortcoming of the target income hypothesis is the lack of an explanation for the income target itself and the specification of the constraints that prevent continuous upward revision of targets. In addition, micro behavioral models (e.g., of utility maximizing physicians) are difficult to test directly.

- Identification problems in econometric models: The discussion has shown, that many tests for SID that can be found in the literature face certain econometric problems. Generally, it is the issue of identification that is most difficult to address satisfactorily. Often identification rests on instruments with uncertain validity or on *a priori* reasoning excluding certain feedback channels. In some cases this is done in a convincing way, like in the case of cesarean deliveries (Gruber and Owings, 1996), where identification is rather plausible. Also some direct evidence, like the comparatively rare cases of gall bladder operations of physicians, is compelling. However, this kind of evidence of inducement is generally limited to a special treatment. Until now it is very hard to come up with an estimate about the impact of SID on aggregate variables.

We have seen that many elements of the agency relationship between physician and patient like reputation, separation, capacity constraint, guilt feelings and/or convex costs can limit opportunistic behavior and therefore demand inducement. Although there is ambiguous empirical support of the inducement hypothesis, one could reasonable conclude that some deviations from perfect agency and therefore demand inducement exist.

In the majority of the health care reforms in the OECD countries the existence of supplier induced demand has been assumed in the debate about the various remuneration systems. By analyzing the different stylized facts of the various markets of health care providers it is necessary not only to precisely investigate the institutional settings of these markets, but also to explicitly model the interactions in these markets. Making the assumptions explicit and deriving equilibrium results is necessary to focus the political debate on the important parts of interest.

We now apply the basic insight gained by the supplier induced demand literature to the budget system.

Chapter 4

Strategic Interaction in the Market for Physician Services: The Treadmill Effect in a Fixed Budget System

4.1 Introduction

In Germany in 1993 in the market for physician services there was a switch from the cost reimbursement system to a remuneration system with a fixed budget to contain health care costs.[74] In this prospective payment system with a fixed total budget the individual physician learns only retroactively how much he has actually earned: He faces the strategic uncertainty how his

---

[74]Some other countries have also gathered some experience with total budgets. Fixed budget systems for example are used in the physician remuneration system of France, the United Kingdom and are also partially used in the U.S.A., i.e. in the Medicare services. Although the federal government in the United States has proposed the option of a fixed budget within the Clinton health plan, global budgets have been introduced only within a small percentage in the health industry in the U.S.A. In Canada since 1990 payment for physician services in the fee-for-service sector has shifted from an open-ended system to fixed global budgets (Hurley and Card, 1996).

professional colleagues act. Looking at the German outpatient market the following interesting observations can be made:

1. Since the 90's the average income of physicians has decreased substantially.[75]

2. Furthermore, since the introduction of the budget system, the point value - the price determined ex post - dropped significantly.[76]

In this chapter we suggest one possible explanation for these observations, and argue how they may be related to each other. For this purpose we investigate the interaction in the market for physician service when the budget is fixed. By analyzing the strategic uncertainty of a single doctor we show that the market for physician service can - due to a coordination problem - be stuck in an equilibrium which involves bankruptcy and therefore market exit. This equilibrium can arise, because - given a certain total budget - physicians have to augment their number of treatments to avoid bankruptcy. As a consequence a downward spiral of prices finally forces some physicians to exit the market. Our analysis suggests that the introduction of a specific mechanism of a price floor into the German market for physician service could solve this coordination problem.

Our model belongs to the field of research where alternative reimbursement schemes are investigated and compared, as discussed in Chapter 3.[77] Consequently a lot of the empirical papers have examined the effects of exogenous changes in physician remuneration programs.[78] However, strategic aspects (in our case induced through a fixed budget) have not been investigated so far.

---

[75]From 1996 to October 1997 the income of physicians in the outpatient service decreased by up to 30 percent (Berliner Morgenpost, 1997).

[76]For instance in 1996 in the south western region of Germany the average value of a point declined by more than 16 percent (Ärzte-Zeitung, 1996).

[77]See also Newhouse (1992) and Ellis and McGuire (1993) for reviews.

[78]For summaries see Rice and Labelle (1989), Dranove and Wehner (1994) and Scott and Hall (1995).

We compare the remuneration system of fee-for-service, what we call price system, with the prospective payment system of a fixed total budget, what we call point system. As described in Chapter 2 in this payment system with ex post prices the individual physician receives a certain number of points per treatment which depends on the kind of service he renders. At the end of each quarter the fixed budget for all physicians is divided by the sum of points submitted by all physicians for reimbursement. Therefore from the point of view of an individual physician the amount he receives from the reimbursement center does not only depend on the sum of points of his treatments but also on the number of treatments of all other doctors in the market. We investigate how physicians act when they are able to control the number of treatments.

In a general model of physician behaviour with a price system we show that physicians maximize their utility, taking into account monetary and effort cost, if prices are high. However, if prices are low, physicians forgo their effort costs to avoid bankruptcy. They expand their treatments to the target where monetary costs will be covered. If prices are getting too low, some physicians are forced to declare bankruptcy.

In contrast to this price system we find that in the budget system there exists a coordination problem. Depending on the size of the budget, the possible equilibria have one of three different structures. If the budget is very high, there exists a unique equilibrium in pure strategies where the individual physician behaves as a profit maximizer. If the budget is very low, there exists a unique equilibrium where a proportion of physicians exit the market and the others work very hard to avoid bankruptcy. In the scenario with an intermediate budget there exist the two equilibrium outcomes as described above and one additional equilibrium with an intermediate price level, where all physicians work hard[79], but there is no market exit. We argue that this last equilibrium is unstable.

---

[79]This phenomenon, where physicians increase their treatments is commonly referred to the term "treadmill effect", see e.g. Breyer (2000).

Physicians do not seem to coordinate themselves on an equilibrium with high prices. We show that there exist two possible coordination devices. First, the physicians are guaranteed that the budget will be augmented if the point-value drops by more than a predetermined percentage. This point value guarantee will not be used in equilibrium and the budget target will be met. Second, alternatively a prospective maximal number of treatments can be implemented into the budget. However, this second coordination device involves high information and administration effort. Finally we analyze the equilibrium when entry into the market is possible. Physician will enter the market only if the budget is large enough and if their utility by entering the market exceeds their outside option. In this case we show that a fixed budget can lead to a desired allocation of human capital.

The chapter is organized as follows. In Section 4.2 a basic model of physician choice where physicians can induce demand is presented. In Section 4.3 we introduce the fixed budget phenomenon into our framework and compare the two different approaches of reimbursement. We study how strategic interaction of physicians leads to a coordination problem. In Section 4.4 we derive ways how to solve the coordination problem. Then, in Section 4.5 market entry of physicians is included into the model. Finally, Section 4.6 concludes.[80]

4.2 The Basic Model

We present a simple model to capture the relevant aspects of the strategic uncertainty in the market for physician service. Especially we draw attention to the different equilibrium outcomes of the two methods of reimbursement, the fee-for-service system, what we call price system, and the prospective payment system with a fixed total budget, which will be called point system.

---

[80]This Chapter is based on the paper "Strategic Interaction in the Market for Physician Services" (with Achim Wambach), which was presented at the EEA conference, held in August/September 2000 in Bozen (Italy).

We start by developing a model of the behaviour of the physician in the price system. To do so, the following assumptions are made:

Assumption 1

1. A physician finances his practice by taking out a loan of size F, which has to be paid back at the end of the period.

2. Running costs consist of monetary costs $c_1(n)$ and effort costs $c_2(n)$, with $c'_i > 0$ and $c''_i > 0$ for $i = 1, 2$. n is the number of treatments.

3. If a physician cannot repay his loan, he faces bankruptcy costs of BK.

At the beginning of the period a physician is confronted with fix costs and other liquidity problems. Physicians require equipment, have to pay rents, pay for their employees, etc. Therefore, as implied by Assumption 1.1, a bank loan of size F is needed to finance his expenditures.[81] For instance, a dentist, who decided to open his own practice in 1998 had to finance an average volume of 548,000 D-Mark.[82]

Assumption 1.2 introduces two sorts of variable costs. The monetary costs $c_1(n)$ have to be paid by the physician, while costs $c_2(n)$ describe the disutility he has from providing the service. This might refer to the time spent on work, the effort he has to put in, etc. For simplicity we only consider a single kind of treatment. In addition the physician is confronted by bankruptcy costs BK (Assumption 1.3), which only occur if he cannot pay back his bank loan F. These costs should also be interpreted as private, monetary and non-monetary costs. In the German system, for example, the license fee will be foregone when the practice of a physician is closed and of course, the physician bears a reputational cost for future working possibilities.[83]

---

[81]Allowing for different F_i for different physicians does not change the basic results, as shown in Chapter 4.3.

[82]HypoVereinsbank (1999)

[83]Modelling bankruptcy costs as private costs is a standard tool in the principal-agent analysis, see e.g. Schmidt (1997).

Following Assumption 1, if p is the price per treatment, the utility of a physician who provides n treatments is given by:

$$\Pi(n) = \begin{cases} pn - c_1(n) - c_2(n) - F & \text{if} \quad pn - c_1(n) \geq F \\ -c_2(n) - BK & \text{if} \quad pn - c_1(n) < F \end{cases} \qquad (4.1)$$

If the physician does not go bankrupt, his utility (profit) is income minus costs. However, in case of bankruptcy all monetary income accrues to the bank, so the physician is left with his effort costs and his private bankruptcy costs.

We now turn to the question on how n, the number of treatments is determined. As an empirical fact we observe that physicians act differently under different reimbursement systems. For instance in Germany the number of treatments without proper medical justification seems to have increased in the last decade. An interesting example are the operations of gall bladders. Between 1990 and 1996 their number had risen by 150 percent through the introduction of outpatient endoscopic operation techniques. However, for the same indication, physicians show a rate of operation which is 84% lower than the rate of the average population.[84] Even the German Society of Radiology claims that in 1998 every second out of 100 million ex-rays was not necessary.

The way to model this observation is however very heterogeneous in the literature, demonstrated in Chapter 3: In one strand of the literature physicians can induce demand directly. They just choose the number of treatments. Here, limits to inducement are given either via target incomes Evans (1974) or because the degree of inducement enters utility negatively (e.g. Evans, 1974, McGuire and Pauly, 1992). Another approach models informational differences explicitly by comparing medical services to credence goods. Examples are Emons (1997), Wolinsky (1993, 1995) and Dranove

---

[84]Speech of the state secretary Christa Nickels at the health care congress on May, 11, 1999 in Heidelberg/Germany.

(1988). We are in line with the first strand. However we do not assume that inducement is limited via an exogenous target income or via a possible negative utility, but by cost of treatment instead.[85] Therefore, in our model physicians have complete control over the number of treatments.

Assumption 2

The choice variable of a physician is n, the number of treatments. The overall supply in the market determines the demand for medical services.

In a more elaborate model one would like to constrain the possibilities to induce demand by informational asymmetries between physician and patient. However, for the purpose of the present paper, it is only required that the physician can induce demand to some degree, so the proposed form of modeling seems appropriate. Under Assumptions 1 and 2 we can now solve the maximization problem of the physician. Depending on the price p, three regions for the optimal number of treatments are obtained.

Proposition 4.1 (Fee for service): *There exists a lower bound $\underline{p}$ and an upper bound $\bar{p}$ with $0 < \underline{p} < \bar{p}$, such that:*

If $\bar{p} \leq p$ the optimal number of treatments $n^*(p)$ is such that the individual physician equates price with marginal costs: $p = c_1'(n^*) + c_2'(n^*)$. An increase in price will lead to an increase in n: $\frac{dn^*(p)}{dp} > 0$.

If $\underline{p} \leq p < \bar{p}$ the optimal number of treatments $n^{**}(p)$ is such that bankruptcy is just avoided: $pn^{**} - c_1(n^{**}) = F$. An increase in price will lead to a decrease in n: $\frac{dn^{**}(p)}{dp} < 0$

If $p < \underline{p}$ the optimal number of treatments $\hat{n}$ is 0 and the individual physician exits the market.

---

[85]Adding that the degree of inducement influences utility negatively would not change the results.

Proof Assume that the bankruptcy constraint of equation 4.1 is not binding. Then maximizing this expression with respect to n yields $p - c'_1(n) - c'_2(n) = 0$. This defines n^* as a function of p. Using the implicit function theorem it follows that $n^{*\prime}(p) = \frac{1}{c_1''(n^*) + c_2''(n^*)}$ which is positive as costs are convex. Therefore, if p is large enough it will hold that $pn^*(p) - c_1(n^*(p)) > F$. This proves the first part of the Proposition.

Define $\bar{p}$ such that $\bar{p}n^*(\bar{p}) - c_1(n^*(\bar{p})) = F$. As $c'_1(n^*(p)) < p$, it follows that for all $p < \bar{p}$, $pn^*(p) - c_1(n^*(p)) < F$. Therefore, as long as p is not too small, the bankruptcy constraint becomes exactly binding and the physician chooses the optimal $n^{**}(p)$ such that $pn^{**}(p) - c_1(n^{**}(p)) = F$. Again, using the implicit function theorem gives $n^{**\prime}(p) = -\frac{n^{**}(p)}{p - c_1'(n^{**}(p))}$. In the region of interest this expression is negative: The physician would never provide so many treatments that the marginal monetary costs exceed the price. Therefore $c'_1(n^{**}(p)) < p$. This proves the second part of the Proposition.

Now define $\underline{p}$ as the largest $p < \bar{p}$ such that either $c_2(n^{**}(\underline{p})) = BK$ or $c'_1(n^{**}(\underline{p})) = \underline{p}$. In the first case, effort costs equal the private bankruptcy costs. Therefore at this price the physician is indifferent between going bankrupt or providing n^{**} treatments. In the latter case, marginal costs equal price. In both cases, if prices fall below $\underline{p}$, the physician will exit the market.[86] Due to the fact that n^{**} increases if the price falls, the physician will exit the market for all $p < \underline{p}$.   Q.E.D.

The implications of Proposition 4.1 can most easily be illustrated by Figure 4.1, which shows the supply curve of the physician.

For high prices, the supply curve is upward sloping. We call this region *Profit maximization*, as the physician behaves here like a standard profit maximizer, equating price with marginal costs. For intermediate prices, the

---

[86]We regard the former scenario, where exit occurs due to large effort costs, as more plausible than the latter one. In general, monetary variable costs are relatively low, see HypoVereinsbank (1998).

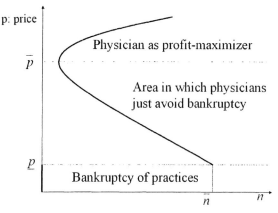

Figure 4.1: The price system

supply curve is downward sloping. To avoid bankruptcy the physician is working harder, even if the price is declining. We call this region *Target income*, as the physician works exactly so much that he covers his bank loan. As mentioned in Chapter 3 there is a long debate in the literature whether the so-called target-income-hypothesis holds. One of the main criticisms with this approach is that the target is not derived, but just postulated. In our model, we obtain for some prices a target-income, with an explicit explanation for the target: For intermediate prices physicians work so much that they cover their costs. Note that one result of this model is that the target is in income, and not in utility.[87] If the price is very low, the physician exits the market and supplies nothing. This is indicated with the bold part of the vertical axis in the graph. We can now turn to the analysis of strategic interaction between physicians under a fixed budget.

---

[87]For the debate about the target income hypothesis see e.g. Labelle, Stoddart, and Rice (1994).

4.3 The Budget System:
Strategic Uncertainty

In this section we investigate the strategic interaction in the market for physician services when the budget is fixed. As described above, in a point system with a global expenditure cap, the value of a point is determined ex-post. It is given by the budget divided through the number of points all physicians accumulate together. We want to capture the strategic element which arises in such a setting. To do so, assume that a continuum of physicians exist. The physicians are indexed by a parameter x which is distributed uniformly on the line $[0,1]$.[88]

Given a budget of size B, the structure of the game is the following:

Each individual physician x decides either to exit the market, which implies that he sets $n(x) = 0$, or he stays in the market and chooses to provide the number of treatments $n(x) > 0$. Depending on the number of treatments chosen by the other physicians $(n(y), y \neq x)$, the pay-offs to physician x are then given by:

$$
\Pi(n(x)) = \begin{cases} \dfrac{B}{\int_0^1 n(y)dy}\, n(x) \; - c_1(n(x)) - c_2(n(x)) - F \\[2ex] \qquad \text{if } \dfrac{B}{\int_0^1 n(y)dy} n(x) - c_1(n(x)) \geq F \\[2ex] -c_2(n(x)) - BK \\[2ex] \qquad \text{if } \dfrac{B}{\int_0^1 n(y)dy} n(x) - c_1(n(x)) < F \end{cases} \qquad (4.2)
$$

The first line of the payoff-function is clear: If the expected price per treatment, given by the expression $\dfrac{B}{\int_0^1 n(y)dy}$, is such that by working $n(x)$ the physician earns enough revenue not to go bankrupt, he obtains his profit minus the effort costs of work. If he goes bankrupt (the second line), all his

---

[88]Using a continuum rather than a discrete number of physicians implies that the individual supply of any physician has no consequence for the resulting point-value. This seems to be a sensible assumption to make, given that e.g. in Germany more than 110.000 physicians are reimbursed by the German reimbursement centers.

monetary return is used to pay for the outstanding loan. So the individual physician is left over with his effort costs and the bankruptcy costs. For the following proposition, we define $\bar{n}$ as the number of treatments a physician supplies if the price is $\underline{p}$ (see Figure 4.1). Recall that $\underline{p}$ was the minimum price at which an individual physician would be willing to stay in the market. Depending on the size of the budget, the possible equilibria have one of three different structures.

Proposition 4.2: *There exists a lower bound $\underline{B}$ and an upper bound $\bar{B}$ for the budget, such that*

If $\underline{B} < B < \bar{B}$ there exist three equilibrium outcomes:

- *$E_1 : \forall x \in [0,1] \ \ n(x) = \arg\max_n [\frac{B}{n(x)} n - c_1(n) - c_2(n)]$*

- *$E_2 : \forall x \in [0,1] \ \ n(x)$ s.t. $\frac{B}{n(x)} n(x) - c_1(n(x)) = F$*

- *E_3: A proportion α of physicians exits the market, and the other physicians provide $\bar{n}$ treatments each. α is determined such that $B = (1 - \alpha)\bar{n}\underline{p}$.*

If $\bar{B} < B$ the unique equilibrium is of type E_1.

If $B < \underline{B}$ the equilibrium outcome is of type E_3.

Proof See Section C.1 in the appendix.

Here we outline the proof. This is done in 5 steps.

First: No physician influences the overall point-value by his own treatments. Therefore, given the strategies of the others, the response function of the physician is identical to the supply function we calculated in the previous section, if we identify the price $\tilde{p}$ on the y-axis with the point-value $\frac{B}{\int_0^1 n(y)dy}$. This supply function is displayed in Figure 4.2.

Second: Assume that $\frac{B}{\int_0^1 n(y)dy} \neq \underline{p}$. Then Figure 4.2 shows that the best response of physician x is uniquely determined. Let this be some $\tilde{n}$. Now

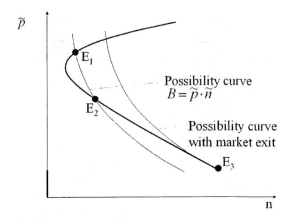

Figure 4.2: The point-system with an intermediate budget

it cannot be the case that any other physician supplies a different number of treatments, because if $\tilde{n}$ is the optimal response for physician x, it must be the optimal response for any other physician. Thus, as long as we are not at the point of indifference between bankruptcy and working hard, the equilibrium strategies must be the same for everyone.

Third: Assume that $\frac{B}{\int_0^1 n(y)dy} = \underline{p}$. In that case physician x is indifferent between working $\bar{n}$ or exiting the market. As this holds for any physician, in equilibrium there might be some physicians who exit the market and some others who supply $\bar{n}$.[89]

Fourth: Now consider the budget. For Figure 4.2 we have chosen the budget such that the line B/n cuts the supply curve twice, at points E_1 and E_2 (the possibility curve to the left). This corresponds to the scenario with an intermediate budget. These two points are two equilibria; if everyone supplies the number of treatments given at these points, then the ex-post price will be such that this number of treatments was individually optimal in the first place. As can be seen from Figure 4.2, either all physicians work less hard and enjoy a large point value (E_1), or all physicians supply more at a lower point value (E_2) and just avoid bankruptcy. If some physicians

---

[89] In general, every physician could mix between exiting or supplying $\bar{n}$.

exit the market the budget line per active physician moves to the right. This is shown by the possibility curve to the right in Figure 4.2 which has the functional form $p = B/((1 - \alpha)n)$. If α is chosen such that this line cuts the point $E_3 = (\bar{n}, \underline{p})$, the third equilibrium is obtained. Some physicians work very hard, the others exit the market, and they are all indifferent between the two alternatives.

Fifth: If the budget is so large that even for $\alpha = 0$ the point $(\bar{n}, \underline{p})$ is not cut, then the only possible equilibrium is the one where all physicians work little and where the price per treatment is very high. This is displayed in Figure 4.3 by the intersection with the line to the right.[90]

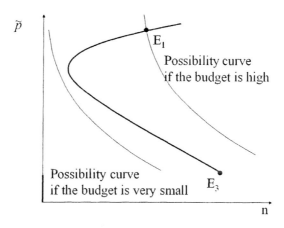

Figure 4.3: The point-system with a high and with a very small budget

If on the other hand the budget is so small that B/n does not even cut the supply curve, (the budget line to the left in Figure 4.3), then the unique equilibrium is the one where some physicians go bankrupt.

For the following discussion we concentrate on the case of an intermediate budget, where all three forms of equilibria exist. The equilibrium at point E_1 in Figure 4.2 is, from the point of view of the physicians, the optimal outcome. Everyone supplies treatment exactly to the point that (expected)

---

[90]Therefore $\bar{B}$ is determined by $\frac{\bar{B}}{\bar{n}} = \underline{p}$.

price equals marginal costs. There is no danger of going bankrupt. The
equilibria in points E_2 and E_3 differ from the first equilibrium in that the
physicians are supplying more treatments: They just avoid bankruptcy while
at equilibrium point E_3 some even exit the market.

These latter two equilibria are however, hard to distinguish empirically.
Remember that we modelled all physicians to have equal cost-functions, and
equal debts to be paid back. If we heterogenize the model, one would also
at equilibrium E_2 expect some of the physicians, namely those with high
costs, to go bankrupt. The main difference between E_2 and E_3 is the nature
of the interaction between the supply of the physicians. By investigating
the sign of the slope of a single physician's reaction function, it is easy to
see, that at the intermediate equilibrium the actions of the physicians are
strategic complements. That is, if any other physician increases his number
of treatments, the point value falls, which makes the individual physician
increasing his treatments as well. In contrast, in equilibrium E_3, if someone
increases the number of treatments, the price falls below the threshold $\underline{p}$
which makes another physician exit the market, which implies a reduction
in in the number of treatments.[91] The strategic complementarity makes the
intermediate equilibrium unstable from a phenomenological point of view.
Consider the case of a "price shock", where everyone believes that the end-
of-year point value is lower. This makes everyone work harder, which results
in even lower prices, and thus finally in some physicians exiting the market.
Thus the intermediate equilibrium would move towards the lower equilibrium.
As mentioned above, we do not think that from an empirical point of view
equilibria E_2 and E_3 differ very much. And, as we will show later on, also
in terms of policy implication it does not matter which of the two equilibria
we consider. Still, due to the instability of the intermediate equilibrium, we
will concentrate in the following only on equilibrium E_1 and E_3. We call

---

[91]It is easy to see that also in equilibrium outcome E_1 the number of treatments are
strategic substitutes.

these the "upper" (coordinated) and "lower" (non-coordinated) equilibrium outcomes, as the physicians strictly prefer to end up in the upper one.

Given the anecdotal evidence we reported in the introduction, it seems to be the case that the German physicians opted for the lower equilibrium. In some sense this choice is understandable: If someone believes that the equilibrium is the upper one, and he supplies less treatments, however the outcome turns out to be the lower one, then he goes bankrupt, which comes with very high costs. Contrary, if the single physician works hard in the belief to be in the lower equilibrium, then, if the outcome is the upper one, he earns more per point than expected and surely does not go bankrupt.[92]

Until now we have assumed that all physicians are the same, so that the model cannot predict who exits the market. However, the model is easily modified to capture some heterogeneity on the side of the physicians. Assume that physicians differ with respect to the size of loans they have to repay. In a price system, for any price p there exists a $\bar{F}(p) > \underline{F}(p)$, such that a physician with an F larger than $\bar{F}(p)$ would exit the market. A physician with an intermediate F, i.e. $\underline{F}(p) < F < \bar{F}(p)$, would work to finance his loan. Finally, those with very small values of F, i.e. if $F < \underline{F}(p)$ would equate price with marginal costs.

The market supply curve now depends on the distribution of F. In Appendix C.2 we provide an explicit example where the market supply curve is decreasing for some range of prices. In that case, if a shift from a price to a point system occurs, three or more equilibria can exist.

Comparing the analogue of the upper and lower equilibrium, the following holds:

Statement (Heterogeneous Physicians) *Let p_1 (p_2) be the price at the upper (lower) equilibrium. Then:*

---

[92]This argumentation is similar to the one used by Harsanyi and Selten (1988) in the discussion of a risk-dominated equilibrium. However, the generalization from a two player game to one with infinitely many players has to be considered as pure analogy, not as theoretically well-defined concept.

Physicians with $F \leq \underline{F}(p_2)$ supply less in the lower equilibrium.

Physicians with $\underline{F}(p_2) \leq F \leq \underline{F}(p_1)$ work harder in the lower equilibrium.

Physicians with $\bar{F}(p_2) < F < \bar{F}(p_1)$ stay in the market in the upper equilibrium, but exit in the lower equilibrium.

This result gives rise to an interpretation if we assume that younger physicians have larger debts to repay. Then if a shift from the upper to the lower equilibrium occurs, one would expect that young physicians exit the market or supply more treatments, while more elderly physicians will supply less treatments. The result is similar if the heterogeneity is in bankruptcy costs, and if the elder physicians have lower bankruptcy costs. Then the elderly physicians will work less in the lower equilibrium. In this case, they might even exit in the lower equilibrium, where prices are low.

Based on the analysis in this section, the following testable predictions about the behaviour of physicians can be made: Assume that in a price system physicians equate price and marginal costs, and that the budget is large enough to cover the expenses of the price system. Then, if the system changes from a price system to a system with a fixed budget, and if the physicians coordinate on the lower equilibrium, we expect that

- the price per treatment, i.e. the point value, declines,

- the net income per physician decreases,

- some physicians will exit the market and others just avoid bankruptcy,

- young physicians work harder or exit the market, while more elderly physicians will work less hard.

4.4 Coordination Mechanisms

To avoid the from the physician's prospective undesired consequences, namely the low outcome, there are two possibilities: First, consider a system where a budget is given, but physicians are guaranteed that the point value will not fall below some prespecified value. If it does, then the budget will be augmented so that every physician obtains this value. Then, for particular values of the size of the budget and the lower point value, the outcome of the game above can be unique:

Lemma 4.1 (Point value guarantee): *In a remuneration system with a fixed budget and an appropriate point value guarantee, such that the budget is augmented if the point value falls below the guaranteed level physicians will coordinate on the upper equilibrium and the budget will be met.*

Proof The proof is done by noting that if the point value guarantee lies above the two lower equilibria of the previous game, then these two can not be equilibrium outcomes anymore. However, the upper, coordinated equilibrium can still be the outcome (and is the unique equilibrium), as here the point value guarantee does not bind. Q.E.D.

This can be seen in Figure 4.4: Due to the price guarantee the budget line has a kink at the level $\check{p}$. If the value of $\check{p}$ is large enough, there is only one intersection of the budget line with the supply-curve. Therefore only the upper equilibrium E_1 exists.

A second possibility to avoid the coordination problem is given by prospectively implementing a maximal number of treatments per physician into the budget system. The number of treatments beyond this predetermined number of treatments per individual physician will not be remunerated by the reimbursement centers:

Lemma 4.2 (Maximal number of treatments): *In a remuneration system with a fixed budget and an appropriately chosen maximal number of*

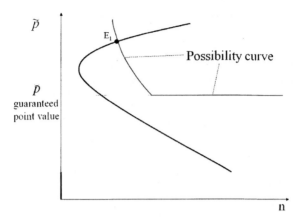

Figure 4.4: The point-system modified by a point value guarantee

treatments per physician, physicians will coordinate on the upper equilibrium and the budget will be met.

Proof To avoid the undesired treadmill effect, this maximal number of treatments per physician ($\check{n}$) has to lie above the two lower equilibria. Like in the case of a point value guarantee, the upper (coordinated) equilibrium can still be the outcome, because in this case the maximal number of treatments does not bind. Q.E.D.

This can be seen in Figure 4.5: Due to the maximal number of treatments for each individual physician, the budget line stops exactly at the level of $\check{n}$. If, given the previous upper equilibrium, the maximal number of treatments is relatively small, there is again only one intersection of the budget line with the supply-curve, the unique equilibrium E_1.

The consequences of either a guaranteed point value or a maximal number of treatments per physician are the same in this model: The undesired treadmill effect can be avoided.

However, if we go beyond the model these two methods of solving the coordination problem become very different. We discuss three effects.

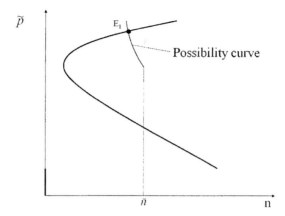

Figure 4.5: The point-system modified by a maximal number of treatments per physician

First, consider the consequences of a health shock, like e.g. an unanticipated wave of influenza. In the case of a predetermined maximal number of treatments per physician there will not be enough supply to treat all patients. In the other case, where a minimal point value is guaranteed, the budget will be augmented and all patients with influenza will be treated.

Second, we also have to take into account that practices vary by size and by the distribution of their patients. Thus implementing a maximal number of treatments per physician requires detailed knowledge of each practices, while a point value guarantee does not need much further information.

A third issue arises if we allow for a dynamic setting. In the system with a guaranteed lower bound on the point value, it might be the case that if physicians fear falling point values and therefore falling income levels in future periods, they will expand their treatments in the present period to cash in today. Thus the budget needs to be augmented. On the other hand, such an effect is not possible in a budget system with a maximal number of treatments per physician and period.

In June 1997 the reimbursement system in Germany shifted from a pure budget to the so-called "Practice-budget", which includes a maximal number of treatments per physician (and which is a budget on points rather than on money). This maximal number depends on the calculated average treatments per group of physicians and on age of the patients. Although this comes close to the system proposed here, it differs in that the point-value is fixed as long as physicians do not reach their limit on the number of treatments. The introduction of this system with a maximal number of treatment came - as discussed before - with huge administrative effort. However, the alternative instrument of a minimum point value would have been more difficult to implement: The German associations for panel doctors would have not only required the agreement by the public sickness fond, they also needed a different legal frame to be provided by the government.

4.5 Market Entry

In this section we extend the model and allow for market entry. The market entry decision is influenced by the payment regime in the (regulated) physicians market and with that by the well-being of the active physicians. As a matter of fact, due to the declining income of physicians more and more young physicians in Germany decide nowadays to work in alternative jobs like in business consulting, hospitals, pharmaceutical industry etc. (compare e.g. Berliner Morgenpost (1999)). We model market entry by introducing a stage 0, in which new physicians (those finishing their "approbation time") can decide to enter the market. For simplicity we assume that if they enter, they also have to repay the debt F in the following period. If they do not enter, they take an alternative job which comes with utility $\hat{U}$, which is assumed to be positive. The stock of possible entrants is given by S^E. We denote the number of entrants in equilibrium by δ. Then, in stage 1, $1 + \delta$ physicians decide simultaneously how many treatments, if any, they supply. Compared to the game in Section 4 the payoff-function has to be redefined, because the number of physicians in stage 1 has now changed to $1 + \delta$.[93] The pay-off for

---

[93] We index the physicians who are in the market at stage 1 by $x \in [0, 1 + \delta]$.

physician x who is in the market in stage 1 and assuming that he does not go bankrupt is given by:

$$\frac{B}{\int_0^{1+\delta} n(y)dy} n(x) - c_1(n(x)) - c_2(n(x)) - F \qquad (4.3)$$

In a regulated system like e.g. the German health market (but also many other health systems) the regulating authority faces two main problems: First, to provide the right incentives for the supply of treatments. Second, to find the right overall reimbursement level for physicians.[94] In contract theory terms: Even if the structure of the second best contracts induced by the incentive constraint is clear, it still needs to be determined how the overall level of the reimbursemt per physician, as spelled out by the participation constraint, is set. In contract theory, it is usually just assumed that a participation constraint exists.[95] In the health sector, there is no obvious level for the size of the participation constraint: How much should a physician earn? What reimbursement induces the right level of entry? Using competitive analysis, one would expect that wage equal to marginal product would be the appropriate payment. Paying more induces excessive entry, while paying less will lead to a reduction in entry (or a shift towards lower quality physicians). One possible indicator for the right payment could be the outside option physicians have. If that market (consulting, pharmaceutical industry) is much less regulated than the health care market, the payment there should be close to productivity. We therefore interpret $\hat{U}$ as the correct overall level of reimbursement for physicians with the following implication: If physicians expect to earn $\hat{U}$ in the market for physician services, the desired number of entry to this market will be induced.[96]

---

[94]While the first question is addressed excessively in the literature (for summary see Gaynor (1994)), the second problem has received very little attention.

[95]E.g. Ma and McGuire (1997) assume a reservation utility for the physician.

[96]In our homogeneous model the following holds: If expected earnings are larger (lower) than $\hat{U}$, all (no) physicians will enter. Both alternatives are suboptimal. Only for expected earnings equal to $\hat{U}$, optimal entry can be expected.

With these preliminaries, the following observation can be made:

Lemma 4.3: *If the equilibrium of the subgame at stage 1 is not the upper one, then no additional physician will enter the market.*

If the equilibrium of the subgame at stage 1 is the upper one, then depending on the size of the budget, either all physicians or no physician enter at stage one, or exactly so many that the expected profit equals the outside option, i.e.

$$\hat{U} = \frac{B}{(1+\delta)n^*}n^* - c_1(n^*) - c_2(n^*) - F \qquad (4.4)$$

where n^* is the equilibrium number of treatments at stage 1.

The reasoning is obvious. Physicians will only enter the market if they expect to obtain more or equal than by staying away. This can only be the case in the upper equilibrium. If the expected profit there without any entry is less than the outside option, no one will enter. If it is larger, then so many physicians will enter until the stock of entrants is exhausted or the expected profit is equal to the outside option. The most interesting case is the latter scenario, where exactly so many physicians enter that their outside option equals the expected profit they obtain in the market itself. Given the remarks above on the interpretation of $\hat{U}$ this implies that market entry is optimal. So, if physicians coordinate on the upper outcome, a fixed budget will lead to an improved allocation of human capital.

This can be seen in Figure 4.6 : Market entry will shift the budget line to the left until the expected profit of the marginal physician, who wants to enter the market, is equal to his outside-option.

This last result points towards the potential a fixed budget has: It might be a useful tool to appropriately regulate market entry. If, as can be assumed, the right size of reimbursement is not known to the government and to the reimbursement center, introducing a budget can be a self-sustaining method to elicit this level of compensation. But, as argued previously, the proposed

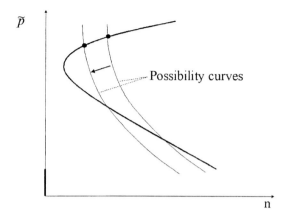

Figure 4.6: The point system can regulate market entry

(improved) budget system can only work properly if sufficient measures are in place to avoid the lower, not coordinated outcome, in which physicians face the "treadmill effect".

4.6 Conclusion

In this chapter we have presented a model of demand inducing physicians which has the property that if prices are high, physicians behave like profit maximizers, while for low prices they behave like satisficers, inducing demand to reach a target income. This target income is given by the monetary costs of the practice. With this model a reimbursement system where the budget is fixed is investigated. Due to a coordination problem physicians may end up in an equilibrium where they have to endure the treadmill effect. The point value falls, the number of treatments increases, and some physicians are forced to exit the market. We provide evidence for these predictions in the German physicians market. However, if physicians succeed to avoid the coordination problem, then a fixed budget has the positive effect that it leads to desired market entry. A possible coordination device could be that to a fixed budget a point value guarantee is added, which in equilibrium will not be used. In our model this coordination device leads to the same result as implementing a prospective maximal number of treatments into the budget system. However, a lower bound on the point-value will establish sufficient health service in case of health shocks and will be much easier to administer. When implementing this measure, however, the government needs to assure to the physician community that it will not cut the budget in future years.

Chapter 5

Risk Sharing between Health Services Purchasers and Providers

5.1 Introduction

In Chapter 4 we investigated the switch from the cost reimbursement to a remuneration system with a fixed budget. Besides the treadmill effect, explored in Chapter 4, risk sharing has heated the debate about whether the government should impose a cap on the expense, i.e. to fix a budget for health care expenditures. To investigate risk considerations we now analyze how health service purchasers (i.e. sickness funds) and providers (i.e. physicians) share risk when different systems of remunerating providers are compared.

While the supporters of the reimbursement system by a fixed overall budget stress the stability of insurance premiums its opponents criticize the negative implications for the physicians in the market for outpatient care. One argument being that in the budget system the morbidity risk (aggregate risk of the population to get ill) is shifted from the health insurance companies to the physicians. If this were the case, then the budget system entails an obvious inefficiency: As health insurer can diversify risks better than individual physicians, any uncontrollable risk should better be levied upon the insurers.

In this chapter we first want to investigate how risks are distributed between the insurers and the physicians in different remuneration systems. In particular we are going to analyze, which of the three payment systems, the budget system, the price system or a fee-per-capita system, will be better if there is uncertainty about the number of people that get ill.[97] Under aggregate risk it turns out that if variable costs are high, the price system fares better. In this case the high (low) earnings one obtains when there are many (few) patients serve as an insurance device against the high (low) costs. On the other hand, if variable costs are low, there is no cost uncertainty. Then the budget system or the fee-per-capita scheme lead to better risk sharing arrangements, because with these remuneration systems the earnings per doctor remain stable independent on the number of patients treated.

In a second step we investigate what consequences a fixed budget has for the interaction between several groups of physicians. We will show that if the number of patients is uncertain, there might be risk and income spillovers as well as possibly income smoothing between different groups of physicians. This observation might help to explain why e.g. in Germany some treatments are paid outside the fixed budget, and why some groups of physicians are more strongly opposed to the budget than others.

The chapter is organized as follows. In Section 5.2 we show how aggregate uncertainty and idiosyncratic risk per doctor about the number of treatments influences the physician's preference for the different reimbursement systems. In Section 5.3 we concentrate on the budget system and show how this system

---

[97]In this chapter we assume that demand for physician services is solely drawn by the number of patients. This is the other extreme compared to Chapter 4. Reality will probably lie somewhere in between.

influences the various groups of doctors in outpatient care differently. Section 5.4 concludes.[98]

5.2 Income Risk under Different Payment Schemes

In this section we concentrate on a simple model where each physician undertakes only one task, and this task is the same for all physicians. The model is generalized in the next section.

We make the following assumptions:
There are k physicians in the market. Each physician i treats $\tilde{y}_i$ patients, where $\tilde{y}_i$ is a random number. Depending on the realization of $\tilde{y}_i$, the costs of treatment are $c(y_i)$.

5.2.1 Aggregate Morbidity Risk

In this subsection we discuss the extreme case where there is only aggregate risk about the number of patients. As an example, consider a wave of influenza which might occur or not.

We specify the model as follows:
Let N be the size of the population, and $\tilde{x}$ be the random proportion of the population which become ill. As all physicians are equal, and as there is only aggregate uncertainty, we can write $\tilde{y}_i = \tilde{y} \equiv \tilde{x}\frac{N}{k}$.

In the price system, there is a fixed price p which will be paid for each treatment. The expected utility of a representative doctor in the price system

---

[98]This Chapter is based on the paper "Risk Sharing between Health Services Purchasers and Providers" (with Achim Wambach).

is then given by:

$$EU^{price} = E[U(p\tilde{y} - c(\tilde{y}))] \tag{5.1}$$

Let us now turn to the budget system, which is also called point-system. Let ϵ denote the number of points per treatment which we normalize to 1, i.e. with one task (treatment) the doctor earns one point. In this point system the budget B is fixed. The ex-ante uncertain value of one point is given by:

$$\tilde{p}_p = \frac{B}{\tilde{x}N} = \frac{B}{k\tilde{y}} \tag{5.2}$$

The point value is equal to the budget divided by the overall number of treatments which is given by $\tilde{x}N$. As there is only aggregate uncertainty this latter expression is equal to the number of physicians times the number of treatments per physician.

For the comparison of the two reimbursement systems we assume that the budget in the point system equals the expected expenditures in the price system: $B = pE[\tilde{x}]N$ or alternatively written: $B = pk\bar{y}$, where $\bar{y} = E[\tilde{y}]$. This implies that the expected income per physician is the same in both reimbursement systems.

With these preliminaries, we can now determine the expected utility for the physician in the point scheme:

$$EU^{point} = E\left[U(\frac{B}{\tilde{x}N}\tilde{y} - c(\tilde{y}))\right] = E[U(p\tilde{y} - c(\tilde{y}))] \tag{5.3}$$

Equations 5.1 and 5.3 allow us to compare the expected utility of the physician between the different regimes. Note that if the health insurer is risk neutral, then she is indifferent between the two payment schemes, as expected payments are the same. Therefore whichever scheme is preferred by the physician will be better overall.

As is clear from equation 5.1, the physician in a price regime faces income risk. If many patients turn up, i.e. y is large, he earns much (py) but has high costs $(c(y))$, while it is the reverse if only a few patients show up in the physician's practice. On the other hand, in the point system the physician only faces cost uncertainty (see equation 5.3). If the number of patients is large, the point value drops so that the product of the number of treatments and of the value of a point remains constant. So his earnings do not increase. But he has large costs. On the other hand, if only a few patients turn up, then, because the uncertainty is global, also the other physicians treat only a few patients, so the point value increases. Therefore his earnings remain at the same level, while he has only small costs of treatment. This analysis suggests that the crucial factors whether the physicians will prefer one or the other payment regime is income uncertainty in a price system versus cost uncertainty. If income uncertainty is large, then probably the budget system fares better, while if cost uncertainty is large, the price system will be preferred.

To make the argument more formal, we make two further simplifying assumptions. First, we assume that costs are linear, i.e. $c(y) = c_f + cy$. Second, we assume that $\tilde{x}$ is uniformly distributed between 0 and x^{up}, where $0 < x^{up} \leq 1$.[99]

The final wealth under the two different regimes as a function of the realization of $\tilde{y}$ are displayed in Figures 5.1 and 5.2. The difference between the two Figures is that in Figure 5.1, $p\bar{y} < (p - c)y^{up}$ holds, while in Figure 5.2 $p\bar{y} > (p - c)y^{up}$, where y^{up} is the upper bound of possible treatments per doctor: $y^{up} = x^{up}N/k$.

As can be seen from the figures, the spread in income under the price system is larger (smaller) in Figure 5.1 (5.2) than under the point system. This gives rise to Proposition 5.1.

---

[99] For our result to hold, we only require that $\tilde{x}$ is symmetrically distributed. See also footnote 100 and in the appendix Chapter D.

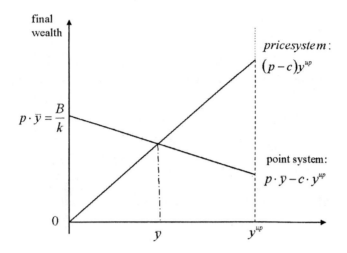

Figure 5.1: Global risk and linear cost function: CASE A: $p\bar{y} < (p - c)y^{up}$

Proposition 5.1: *Under aggregate risk, and given our assumptions*

(i) *any risk averse physician would prefer the point system to the price system if $p - c > c$.*

(ii) *any risk averse physician would prefer the price system to the point system if $p - c < c$.*

Proof [100] We only proof part (i), part (ii) works analogue. In Figure 5.3 we have drawn the probability distribution functions of the physician's earnings in the price system and the point system for case (i). Due to the assumption on the size of the budget, both distributions of the final wealth have the same mean. This implies that the areas A and B have the same size, which

---

[100]We proof this proposition for uniformly distributed $\tilde{x}$. In the Appendix we show that the same proposition holds for any symmetrically distributed $\tilde{x}$.

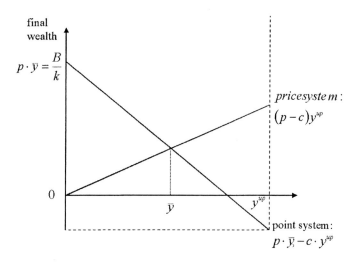

Figure 5.2: Global risk and linear cost function: CASE B: $p\bar{y} > (p - c)y^{up}$

in turn implies that the wealth distribution in the point system (F_2) second order stochastically dominates the distribution in the price system (F_1). As Rothschild and Stiglitz have shown (Rothschild and Stiglitz (1970)), this is equivalent to saying that all risk averse individuals will prefer distribution F_2 to distribution F_1.

The condition for this to be the case is that $p\bar{y} < (p - c)y^{up}$. As $\bar{y} = y^{up}/2$, we have $1/2p < p - c$ which is equivalent to $p - c > c$.   Q.E.D.

If c is relatively small, i.e. if variable costs are small, then the physician prefers the budget system to the price system. In that case, costs are relatively independent on the number of treatments, and the budget system keeps the earnings stable. In other words, the physician is insured against few patients turning up. On the other hand, if c is large (and $p - c$ small), the price system will be preferred. In that case, the increase in earnings if the number of treatments increases is an insurance against the accompanying increase in costs.

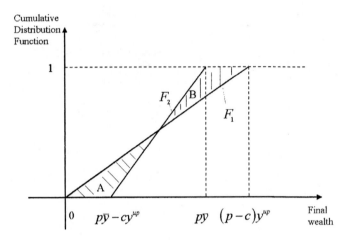

Figure 5.3: Cumulative distribution and final wealth

As a limit result, the following observation can be made:

Remark 1 If the pricing is competitive $(p = c)$, the physicians will prefer the price system.   □

In this case there is no income risk, as income will be zero independent of the number of treatments.[101]

Before we compare these remuneration system with the fee-per-capita scheme, let us first discuss idiosyncratic risk.

5.2.2   Idiosyncratic Risk

In this subsection we turn to the other extreme, where each physician faces an independent uncertainty about the number of patients, while the overall proportion of society which becomes ill is fixed. As an example take local viruses, which influence the number of patients for some (one) physicians, but not for all.

---

[101] For such a regime to be feasible it would be required that there are no fix costs.

Table 5.1: Physicians' income under different remuneration systems

remuneration system / risk	aggregate risk	idiosyncratic risk
fee-for-service	$p\bar{y} - c(\tilde{y})$	$p\bar{y} - c(\tilde{y})$
budget system	$p\bar{y} - c(\tilde{y})$	$p\bar{y} - c(\tilde{y})$
capitation system	$p\bar{y} - c(\tilde{y})$	$p\bar{y} - c(\tilde{y})$

Formally, we assume that $\tilde{y}_i$ is iid for all i, while $\tilde{x} = x$ is constant.[102]

The analysis is now easily done. Due to the feature that we have only idiosyncratic risk, and the overall number of treatments is certain, the price per treatment will be certain, even in the point system. If the budget is chosen such that the (certain) expenditures in both regimes are the same, then the point value will equal the price per treatment. Therefore the physicians (as well as the insurers), will be indifferent between the two systems.

5.2.3   Comparing Reimbursement Schemes

Now we can summarize and evaluate the effects for physicians by comparing the remuneration systems of fee-for-service, fixed budget and capitation. In a capitation system, the physician receives a certain amount of money per patient independent whether he or she turns up at the physician or not. In effect this works like a budget which is distributed among the physicians independent of the actual workload. To compare the systems, we assume that the payment to the physician in the capitation system equals the expected payment in the price system. The payoff to the physician is displayed in Table 5.1.

---

[102]Mathematically this can be obtained if the physicians are uniformly distributed on a line, say $[0, k]$. If $y(x)$ is the realization of $\tilde{y}$, and $\bar{y} = E[y(x)]$, then it holds: $\int_0^k y(x)dx = \int_0^k E[y(x)]dx = x \cdot N$.

To summarize the results: The optimal payment system depends on whether first, there is aggregate or idiosyncratic risk, and second, whether income in the price system is more or less uncertain than costs. If costs are relatively certain, i.e. if variable costs are low, then a system which guarantees a stable revenue is optimal. If there is aggregate risk, this can be achieved by either a budget system or by capitation. If the risk is idiosyncratic, then only capitation will do. On the other hand, if costs are uncertain, i.e. variable costs are high, then the physician will prefer the price system, or, in the case of idiosyncratic risk, also the budget system.

So far we have only considered one group of physician. However, if the riskiness in the number of patients differs between different groups of physicians, then in a budget system (but not in a price or capitation system), there might be spillover effects between groups. That is where we turn to now.

5.3 Further Risk Considerations in the Budget System

In this section we discuss how a budget system might lead to spillovers of income and risk between different groups of physicians. Assume that there are two groups of physicians, which supply different treatments due to their different medical training. Then we can observe two different kinds of phenomena which will be explained in the following subsections:

5.3.1 Risk Spillovers

It is quite obvious that the risk in the number of patients by one group of physician which influences the value of a point can spill over to another group: If, for example, the first group has many patients, this will lead to a lower point value also for the other group.

We characterize two dimensions along which one group might feel disadvantaged through risk spillovers.

Little versus Much Risk

Suppose that one group of physician has low uncertainty about the number of treatments, while the other has a large uncertainty. To go to the extreme, assume that the first group is certain about the number of treatments. If the two different kind of doctors are reimbursed out of the same budget, also the income of the first group will be uncertain. So we expect that after introduction of a budget the income of a group which was relatively stable before becomes more variable.

Interestingly, we do observe in the German health care market that special budgets for very volatile parts of the outpatient market like the emergency rooms of hospitals or the outpatient centers of university hospitals are set aside. This might be due to risk spillovers, as a separate budget for this volatile kind of treatments gives the other groups of physicians more income certainty.

Small versus Big Doctor's Practices

If there is a huge difference of revenue between groups of physicians or even between individual physicians, another kind of risk spillover occurs. The argument is the following: Suppose there are two groups of physicians, the first of which has on average twice as much revenue than the second. Now, if there are ten percent more treatments in the first group, the overall number of treatments increases by 6.67%, which reduces the point value by 6.25%. If however the number of patients of the second group increases by ten percent, this will only increase the overall number of treatments by 3.33%, which in turn reduces the point value by 3.22%. Thus, while variations in the number of patients for the large group of physicians has a strong impact on the smaller group, variations in the latter group do not influence the point value very much.

There might be several reasons why the expected value of revenue for different kind of physicians differs. For instance some physicians are more specialized and receive more points per treatment, others will get more treatments because of better quality, because of a higher number of potential patients etc.

5.3.2   Income Spillovers

Besides the spillover of risks in the budget system there is another kind of spillover when different (groups of) physicians provide different kind of treatments: Income spillovers.

Expected Income Spillovers

Consider again an extreme case where one group of physicians has a certain number of treatments, while the second group faces uncertainty. Normalize the points per treatment for group 1 to 1, i.e. $\epsilon_1 = 1$. If y_1 is certain, then the expected income for group 1 is given by:

$$EI_1 = E\left[\frac{B}{k_1 y_1 + \epsilon_2 k_2 \tilde{y}_2} y_1\right] \tag{5.4}$$

where k_i is the number of physicians in each group, and the expectation is taken with respect to $\tilde{y}_2$.

Assume that the budget is equal to the expected expenditure in the price system, i.e. $B = k_1 p_1 y_1 + k_2 p_2 \bar{y}_2$ and that the relative point value equal the relative prices: $\epsilon_2 = p_2/p_1$. Then it follows that

$$EI_1 = E[\frac{k_1 y_1 + k_2 p_2/p_1 \bar{y}_2}{k_1 y_1 + k_2 \epsilon_2 \tilde{y}_2}] p_1 y_1 > p_1 y_1 \tag{5.5}$$

The latter inequality holds as $\frac{1}{c+x}$ is convex in x and because Jensen's inequality implies $E[f(x)] > f(E[x])$ for any convex f.

Therefore the group with less uncertainty will increase its expected income if a shift from the price system to a budget system occurs.

The intuition for this result is the following: If only a few patients show up by the physicians of group 2, the point value increases, and group 1 with the certain number of treatments almost gets the whole budget. However, if group 2 treats more patients than average, the reduction in the point value will be shared by both groups of physicians.

Therefore we can prospect that within the budget system the income of physicians with more certain treatments rises, whereas the income of physicians who face fluctuations in their number of treatments decreases. For the latter result recall that the expected expenditures remain constant.

Income Smoothing

Another effect which might occur in a budget system with different groups of physician is income smoothing.

Consider two (groups of) physicians with a negative correlation of the number of treatments. Again, take an extreme case where the number of patients is perfectly negatively correlated, i.e. $\tilde{y}_2 = z - \tilde{y}_1$, were z is some constant.

Then, the uncertain income of one (group of) physician is given by:

$$I_1 = \frac{B}{\tilde{y}_1 + \epsilon_2 \tilde{y}_2} \tilde{y}_1 - c(\tilde{y}_1) = \frac{B}{\epsilon_2 + (1 - \epsilon_2)\tilde{y}_1} \tilde{y}_1 - c(\tilde{y}_1)$$

The variability in $\tilde{y}_1$ in the numerator is (partially) compensated through the variability in the denominator.

The intuition for this effect is as follows: Many patients in the budget system lead to a loss due to the reduced point value. If the other group of physicians have a relatively low number of patients this loss will be counterbalanced. The reduction of the point value will be reduced and vice versa, which leads to a smoothing of the physicians' income.

5.4   Conclusion

In this chapter we have discussed the risk sharing arrangements between physicians and health insurers under different payment regimes.

We show that the budget system does not - as it is often postulated - shift the risk only to the physicians. In the system of a fixed budget the remuneration to a physician is relatively independent to the morbidity risk. In the areas of outpatient care, where the proportion of the variable costs to the total costs is relatively small, where rent, labor costs and interest make up the main part of the total costs, a fixed budget system is preferred to the fee-for-service system because the budget is an insurance against relative strong variations in income. However, if variable costs determine the main part of the physician's total costs, the fee-for-service system serves through an increased income by a higher number of treatments as an insurance against falling income through rising treatment costs and therefore is - from the viewpoint of a physician - preferred to the budget system.

Chapter 6

Empirical Evidence in the German Market for Physician Services

Using data from the German outpatient market we present empirical evidence for our model of Chapter 4. Because the German remuneration system changed in 1993 from a fee-for-service system to a system with a fixed budget, and we assume that the physicians have coordinated on the lower equilibrium, we expect that

1. the price per treatment, i.e. the point value, has declined,

2. the net income per physician has gone down,

3. some physicians exited the market and others just avoided bankruptcy.

The first prediction of the model is strongly supported by data from the German Federal Association of Panel Doctors. The graph in Figure 6.1 shows that with the switch from the fee-for-service system to the budget system on January 1, 1993, the point value (without prevention, laboratory

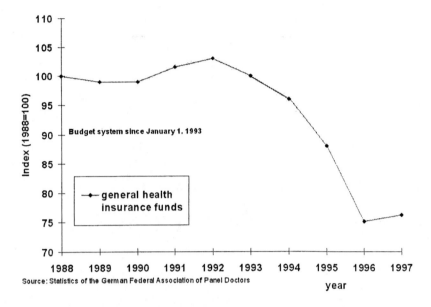

Figure 6.1: Point value development 1988-1997

and outpatient surgery) went on a negative trend. The data is provided by the Bavarian Association of Panel Doctors. Until the end of 1992 the point value was relatively stable because the price was determined ex ante in the fee-for-service system. In 1993 however the point value began to decline rapidly. The point value for all associations of panel doctors fell by about 25% between 1993 and 1997 for the general health insurance funds (Allgemeine Ortskrankenkassen).[103] The introduction of a maximal number of points per practice in 1997 achieved a partial stabilization of the point value.

Also the second hypothesis is supported by the data. This is shown in Figure 6.2 on the basis of the data provided by the Bavarian Association of Panel Doctors. Nominal income peaks in 1992 and real income is more or less

---

[103]The point value for the substitute health insurance funds (Ersatzkassen) dropped by the same amount. Both groups, general and substitute health insurance funds counted together for more than 80% of the funding of the German public market for ambulatory physicians. To see how the population is distributed on the various insurance funds see Section 2.1 and Federal Association of Panel Doctors (1999, Table G17).

constant between 1988 and end of 1992.[104] During the period between 1993
and 1997 the physicians' average nominal income dropped by about 8% and
their income in real terms declined by about 16%.

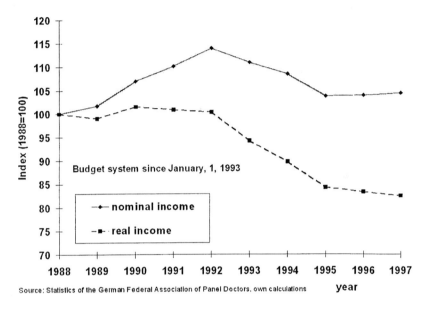

Figure 6.2: Real and nominal physicians' income 1988-1997

This can also be seen in Table 6.1, which summarizes the analysis of cost
and income structure, data collected by the Central Research Institute
of Ambulatory Health Care in Germany (related to the German Federal
Association of Panel Doctors) and by the consulting firm GEBERA.[105] Each
year 2000-2500 physicians respond to an annual survey sent out to about
20% of all physicians, chosen randomly. The survey contains data on the
income situation and cost structure of the German outpatient market.[106]

---

[104]To adjust for inflation the consumer price index for families with higher income was
used.
[105]See also Deutsches Ärzteblatt (1997).
[106]See Zentralinstitut (1988-1998).

Table 6.1: Changes in physicians' income in West Germany

	mean 1990 to 1992		mean 1993 to 1995		value change	
	mean/DM	%	mean/DM	%	% △	% △ p.a.
revenue from						
outpatient care	368,418	80.7	375,512	80,2	1.9	0.6
other revenues	87,945	19.3	92,240	19.8	4.9	1.6
total revenue	**456,363**	**100.0**	**467,752**	**100.0**	**2.5**	**0.8**
costs						
labor costs	112,740	43.6	125,480	44.5	11.3	3.6
other costs	146,110	56.4	156,484	55.4	7.1	2.3
total costs	**258,850**	**100.0**	**281,964**	**100.0**	**8.9**	**2.9**
total costs in						
% of revenue		**56.7**		**60.3**	**6.3**	**2.1**
surplus	**197,513**		**185,788**		**-6.0**	**-2,0**

Source: Statistics of the ZI, own calculations

The table compares revenue and cost figures in a three year period before the reform with a three year period after the reform. The first lines of the table show that the reform did not lead to declining revenues. The revenue from outpatient care rose by 1.9% and other revenues rose by 4.9%, leading to an increase in total revenues by 2.5%. Other revenues have been mainly made up by treatments of privately insured patients (with a fee-for-service system) and by treatments which are not listed in the uniform evaluation standard, which describes the outpatient services reimbursed by the reimbursement center in the budget system.

However, at the same time, total monetary expenditures went up rapidly. On average they increased by about 8.9% between these two periods. The driving force being labor expenditures which rose by 11.3%. As a result, the ratio of total expenditures to revenues rose from 56.7% to 60.3%. In terms of surplus, defined as revenue minus costs, this amounts to a decline of about 6% between the average of 1990-1992 and the average of 1993-1995 .

The third hypothesis is by nature hard to test. Although bankruptcies can be detected - and there are not very many -, surviving at the margin of bankruptcy is hard to find out. Still, there is anecdotical evidence for a increasing number of practices which seem to exist at the margin to survive: This "critical frontier" with a turnover of less than 120,000 Deutsch Marks confronts 6,600 physicians out of 110,000 in outpatient care (Handelsblatt, 1999).

To summarize, empirical data is in agreement with the hypothesis of the theory, although more detailed information is needed to test the theory.

Chapter 7

Outlook

This thesis has investigated and compared alternative physician reimbursement systems, with a focus on overall budgets and their policy implications. We have analyzed how physician reimbursement affects physicians' behavior and how it influences the distribution of risks between physicians and sickness funds. As the most relevant aspects in the market for physician services revolve around information asymmetries, multiple agency and risk sharing, and as technological progress plays an important role in health care expenditures, future research in the following areas as well as empirical work appears to be of particular importance:

Information Asymmetries, Multiple Agency Relationships and Risk Sharing: Patients are generally covered by health insurance, which gives rise to ex post moral hazard. Health insurance funds have to manage ex post moral hazard in the agency relationship with their patients as well as supplier induced demand in the relationship with the health care providers. A complete model would incorporate all these interactions and the form of contracts between the participants would depend on the market structure in all of these markets. A first step in that direction are the papers of Ellis and McGuire (1990) and Ma and McGuire (1997). However, much more work remains to be done to understand these multiple agency relationships as informational asymmetries between physicians and patients are not considered explicitly in these models.

Technological Change in Health Care: Besides the informational asymmetries, health care is a technically complex commodity. Despite the benefits of medical technology it is widely argued that the growth of this technology is a primary cause of rising health care costs in the industrialized countries. However, it is not well understood whether this progress in technology is necessarily welfare improving or not. Due to moral hazard and supplier induced demand one might well observe that welfare reducing technology is implemented. Weisbrod (1991) has discussed the relationship of insurance and technological change. However, the interactions between supplier induced demand and technological change have not received much attention.

Empirical Research: Besides a more comprehensive theoretical analysis there are also several empirical questions that need to be investigated. Most importantly, as emphasized earlier, an estimate of the influence of reimbursement contracting on physicians' behavior is necessary to derive the adequate policy implications. As discussed in Chapter 3.3 it is rather difficult to properly identify the effect of supplier induced demand on aggregate variables. Especially for the German market for physician services the existing evidence is very weak. A promising research strategy would be to use existing aggregate data on the number of physician visits as well as the total number of points achieved by the various groups of physicians to calculate the content of an average visit.[107] It would then be possible to estimate the influence of physician availability, physician income etc. on this variable in a cross section and/or time series setting.[108]

To examine inducement for particular treatments, there is the need for more micro level data on the physician and patient level. With a matched

---

[107]The idea is similar to the study of Birch (1988) for U.K. dentistry.

[108]But even if SID doesn't play a significant role for aggregate budgets this does not mean that it can be neglected. Welfare losses due to inappropriate treatments can be much higher than the unnecessary costs caused by inducement.

physician-patient data set it is a straightforward exercise to study systematic effects of physician characteristics on the choice of treatment. If there exist only a few possible treatments for a certain diagnosis it is possible to relate the proportion of more profitable treatments, from the physician's view, to physician income, for example. A good example is the study of Gruber and Owings (1996) examining cesarean deliveries. Similar estimations could be made for many other treatments, if data were available. Unfortunately, in Germany because of the strict separation of the organizations of physicians and the insurance funds and because the regional associations of panel doctors reimburse the total budget to the physicians, it is difficult to get micro data on physicians.

To summarize, health economics and in particular the behavior of physicians is a relevant and exciting topic. Although our understanding has improved strongly over the last twenty years, still more work has to be done to understand this market.

Appendix A

Appendix of Chapters 1 and 2

Figure A.1

By international comparison, Germany's health care system is expensive, both in absolute terms shown in figure A and as a percentage of gross domestic product which was shown in Table 1.1. With US $ PPP 2364 per capita total expenditures on health care in Germany lie fare above the EU average of US $ PPP 1771.

Figure A.2

Figure A.2 in this appendix chapter shows all major actors as well as their main interrelationships in the German health care market with the focus on the market for physician services and the hospital market.

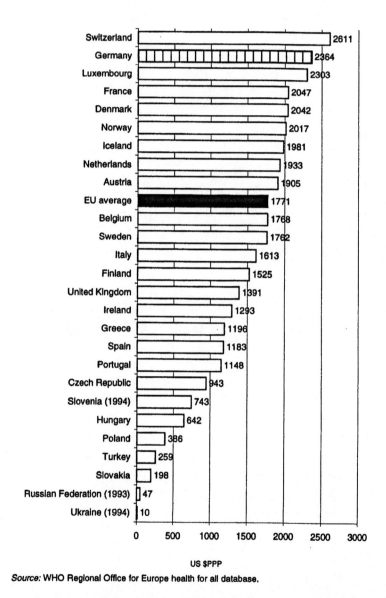

Figure A.1: Total expenditure on health care in the WHO European region (US $ PPP per capita), 1997 or latest available year

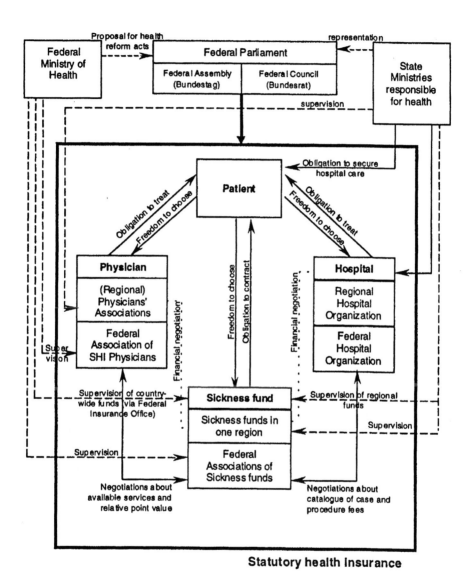

Figure A.2: The organizational relationships of the major actors in the German health care market with focus on the market for physician services and the hospital market

Appendix B

Appendix of Chapter 3

B.1 Investigation of the First Order Condition: Equation 3.14
Proof that $D \geq 0$ in an Optimum

We investigate the case where $v(D)$ is not differentiable at $D = 0$, where again $v(D)$ has the properties: $v'' \geq 0 \ \forall \ D \neq 0$, $v' > 0 \ \forall \ D > 0$, $v' < 0 \ \forall \ D < 0$, $v(D) \geq 0$, $v(D) \geq 0$, (also stated in footnote 57).

Proposition B.1: *In an optimum, D is always non-negative: $D \geq 0$. Depending on the shape of the function $v(D)$, $D > 0$ or $D = 0$.*

Proof Assume that $D < 0$. The Kuhn-Tucker condition for a maximum with respect to D subject to the constraint $D \leq 0$ is:

$$PRf_D - C'Rf_D - v'(D) \geq 0, D \leq 0$$
$$[PRf_D - C'Rf_D - v'(D)] \cdot D = 0 \tag{B.1}$$

We know that $R \cdot f_D > 0$, $(P - C') > 0$ and $v'(D) < 0 \ \forall \ D < 0$. Therefore $PRf_D - C'Rf_D - v'(D) > 0$ for $D < 0$, contradicting the Kuhn-Tucker condition (complementary slackness). Hence, if D is constrained to be non-positive, the only optimal choice is $D = 0$.   Q.E.D.

The physician would never choose $D < 0$.

Intuition: A negative D decreases (as well as a positive D) the utility because of "moral reasons". Furthermore $D < 0$ means less demand and therefore a smaller action space (price-quantity space).

Maximizing with respect to D under the constraint $D \geq 0$ then leads to the Kuhn-Tucker condition

$$PRf_D - C'Rf_D - v'(D) \leq 0, D \geq 0$$
$$[PRf_D - C'Rf_D - v'(D)] \cdot D = 0. \tag{B.2}$$

At least one of the two inequalities must bind (with equality). We know from the first order condition for P that $(P - C') > 0$.

Let $D = 0$. Since $f_D > 0$, it follows $f_D(P, 0) > 0$. So $Rf_D(P - C') > 0$ for $D = 0$.

Finally we have to check the shape of $v(D)$. If $\lim_{\delta \to 0+} \frac{v(0+\delta)-v(0)}{\delta} \equiv v'(0^+) = 0$, in words, if the marginal disadvantage of the first unity of D is zero, then $\lim_{D \to 0+}[Pf_D(P, D)(P - C') - v'(D)] = Pf_D(P, 0)(P - C') > 0$, which contradicts the Kuhn-Tucker condition for optimality. Hence it must be that $D > 0$.

Intuition: With the first marginal unit of the change in D, there is no utility loss, but higher demand. Therefore for the physician it is always optimal to induce more demand as he gets more action room in the price-quantity space. When the physician can increase demand without involving costs, he has a dominant strategy to do this.

If, instead, $\lim_{\delta \to 0+} \frac{v(0+\delta)-v(0)}{\delta} \equiv v'(0^+)$ is sufficiently positive, then $\lim_{D \to 0+}[Pf_D(P, D)(P - C') - v'(D)] < 0$, and it is optimal to choose $D = 0$ according to the Kuhn-Tucker-condition.

Intuition: If $v'(0^+)$ is sufficiently large, the advantage out of increased demand and hence profits due to the very first unit of D is smaller than the disadvantage out of $-v(D)$.

B.2 Comparative Statics

Starting with equation 3.13, the first order condition for P, and differentiating totally we get:

$$R \cdot [f_P + f_P + Pf_{PP} - C''Rf_P^2 - C'f_{PP}]dP + R \cdot [f_D + Pf_{PD}$$
$$- C''Rf_Df_P - C'f_{PD}]dD + [f + Pf_P - C'f_P - RC''ff_P]dR = 0 \tag{B.3}$$

Using the FOC for P: $(f + Pf_P - C'f_P = 0)$ and rewriting terms we get the following result:

$$R \cdot [2f_P - C''Rf_P^2 + f_{PP}(P - C')]dP + R \cdot [f_D -$$
$$C''Rf_Df_P + f_{PD}(P - C')]dD = R \cdot [C''ff_P]dR \tag{B.4}$$

Now we totally differentiate the FOC for D (equation 3.14):

$$[Rf_D(1 - C''Rf_P) + Rf_{PD}(P - C')]dP + [Rf_{DD}(P - C')$$
$$- R^2C''f_D^2 - v'']dD = [C''Rff_D - f_D(P - C')]dR \tag{B.5}$$

We see that it is not easy to determine the signs of the individual elements. To simplify, we assume that there is a demand function which is linear in P and D. Hence $f(P, D)$ becomes:

$$f(P, D) = \alpha - \beta P + \gamma D \tag{B.6}$$

with $\alpha, \beta, \gamma > 0$.

So $f_P = -\beta < 0$, $f_D = \gamma > 0$ and $f_{PP} = f_{DD} = f_{PD} = 0$.

Given this linear demand function, equations B.4 and B.5 become

$$\underbrace{\begin{pmatrix} a_{11} & a_{12} \\ a_{21} & a_{22} \end{pmatrix}}_{H} \begin{pmatrix} dP \\ dD \end{pmatrix} = \begin{pmatrix} b_1 dR \\ b_2 dR \end{pmatrix} \tag{B.7}$$

where

$$a_{11} = -R[2\beta + C'' R\beta^2] < 0$$
$$a_{12} = R[\gamma + C'' R\beta\gamma] > 0$$
$$a_{21} = R\gamma + R^2 C'' \beta\gamma = R[\gamma + C'' R\beta\gamma] = a_{12} > 0$$
$$a_{22} = -R^2 C'' \gamma^2 - v'' < 0$$
$$b_1 = -C'' R f(P, D)\beta \equiv -C'' N\beta$$
$$b_2 = C'' R f(P, D)\gamma - \gamma(P - C')$$

Let us first calculate the determinant of the Hessian:

$$\det H \equiv \triangle = a_{11}a_{22} - a_{12}a_{21}$$
$$= (-R)[2\beta + C'' R\beta^2][-R^2 C'' \gamma^2 - v''] - [\gamma + C'' R\beta\gamma]^2 R^2 \tag{B.8}$$

By multiplying and rearranging terms we get:

$$\det H \equiv \triangle = [\beta v''[RC''\beta + 2] - R\gamma^2]R \tag{B.9}$$

We assumed that a maximum exists. This implies that $a_{11} < 0, \triangle > 0$. Thus we require:

$$\beta v''[RC''\beta + 2] > R\gamma^2 \tag{B.10}$$

Turning back to comparative statics, we can establish by use of Cramer's rule the change in D due to a change in R.[109]

$$\frac{dD}{dR} = \frac{1}{\triangle}[a_{11}b_2 - a_{21}b_1] \tag{B.11}$$

$$\frac{dD}{dR} = \frac{1}{\triangle}[(-2\beta - C''R\beta^2)[C''Rf\gamma - \gamma(P - C')]R + R[\gamma + C''R\beta\gamma]C''Rf\beta] \tag{B.12}$$

$$\frac{dD}{dR} = \frac{\beta\gamma[(P - C')(C''R\beta + 2) - C''Rf]}{\beta v''[RC''\beta + 2] - R\gamma^2} \tag{B.13}$$

The numerator is negative if $(P - C')(C''R\beta + 2) - C''Rf < 0$.

Finally we turn to the reaction of the price P:

$$\frac{dP}{dR} = \frac{1}{\triangle}[a_{22}b_1 - a_{12}b_2] \tag{B.14}$$

$$\frac{dP}{dR} = \frac{1}{\triangle}[(R^2C''\gamma^2 + v'')C''f(P, D)\beta$$
$$- (\gamma + C''R\beta\gamma)(C''Rf(P, D)\gamma - \gamma(P - C'))]R$$

Rewriting terms, we get:

$$\frac{dP}{dR} = \frac{\overbrace{v''C''f\beta}^{(+)} + \overbrace{\gamma^2(1 + C''R\beta)}^{(+)}\overbrace{(P - C')}^{(+)} - \overbrace{C''\gamma^2Rf(P, D)}^{(+)}}{\beta v''[RC''\beta + 2] - R\gamma^2} \gtrless 0. \tag{B.15}$$

---

[109]Since $\triangle \neq 0$, H is non-singular and the implicit function theorem applies.

Appendix C

Appendix of Chapter 4

C.1 Proof of Proposition 4.2

Let $n(y), y \neq x$ be the equilibrium strategies of the physicians apart from physician x. Define p as $p = \frac{B}{\int_0^1 n(y)dy}$ where we set some finite $n = n(x)$. Note that p is independent of $n(x)$ as long as it is finite. Then the pay-offs for physician x as a function of $n(x)$ is given by:

$$\Pi(x) = \begin{cases} pn(x) - c_1(n(x)) - c_2(n(x) - F & \text{if} \quad pn(x) - c_1(n(x)) \geq F \\ -c_2(n(x)) - BK & \text{if} \quad pn(x) - c_1(n(x)) < F \end{cases}$$

$$(C.1)$$

But this is exactly the same profit function as was derived in the Chapter 4.2 on the price system. The optimal $n(x)$ is the chosen analogue to the derivation in the proof of Proposition 4.1. Thus we can interpret the supply function as the response function of the individual physician. The next steps are straightforward: Note that for any 'price' $p = \frac{B}{\int_0^1 n(y)dy}$ there is a unique best response of physician x as long as $p \neq \underline{p}$. We call this $n(p)$. The same argument applies for the other physicians. Therefore in the equilibrium all physicians supply the same number of treatments. An equilibrium of such a form exists if and only if one can find a value for p such that $p = \frac{B}{n(p)}$. We return to the issue of existence below.

Consider now the case where the 'price' $p = \frac{B}{\int_0^1 n(y)dy}$ is equal to $\underline{p}$. Then the best response of physician x is either to work very hard, i.e. to choose $n = \bar{n}$, or to exit the market, i.e. to choose $n = 0$. The same reasoning applies for all physicians, so such an equilibrium price exists if one can find an α with $0 \leq \alpha < 1$ such that $\underline{p} = \frac{B}{(1-\alpha)\bar{n}}$. If α is strictly larger than zero, then some physicians go bankrupt in equilibrium.[110] Having shown the form of the possible equilibria, we now turn to existence.

Consider first the case where all physicians supply the same number of treatments. This can only be an equilibrium if $p = \frac{B}{n(p)}$, or, in other words, if the line B/n cuts the supply line for the individual doctor (see Figure 4.2 and Figure 4.3). It is obvious that if B is very small such a crossing will not occur (the possibility curve to the left in Figure 4.3). Therefore $\underline{B}$ is defined such that the line $\underline{B}/n$ just touches the supply curve. On the other hand, if B is very large (the possibility curve to the right in Figure 4.3), it crosses the supply curve only once in the region where supply is increasing in p. Accordingly, $\bar{B}$ is defined such that $\bar{B}/\bar{n} = \underline{p}$, i.e. the two curves touch at the point where the physicians just avoid bankruptcy. For all intermediate levels of B there are at least two crossing points (as shown in Figure 4.2).

We now proof that there are at most two crossing points: It is obvious that in the region of the supply curve where n increases in p the two curves can cross at most once, as B/n is decreasing in n. It remains to show that also in the region where n decreases with p at most one crossing occurs. Suppose the two curves cross at a point $p = B/n = (F + c_1(n))/n$. The slopes of the two curves at this point are given by $-B/n^2 = -p/n$ versus $-(F + c_1(n))/n^2 + c_1'(n)/n = -p/n + c_1'/n$. Therefore the budget curve will

---

[110]There are several possible equilibrium strategies which would lead to this result: Either all physicians mix between exiting the market and working hard with probability $(\alpha : 1 - \alpha)$, or a proportion α of physicians with say $x \leq \alpha$ exit the market, the others work hard, etc. The equilibrium outcome, however, has always the same structure.

always decrease more than the supply curve, which in turn implies that there is at most one crossing in this region. Finally, it remains to show that an equilibrium, where some α physicians go bankrupt, exist. By the definition of $\bar{B}$ it is clear that for all $B \leq \bar{B}$ one can always find a $0 < \alpha < 1$ such that $\underline{p} = \frac{B}{1-\alpha} \bar{n}$ holds.

Q.E.D.

C.2 Downward Curving Supply with Heterogeneous Physicians

Physicians differ with respect to the size of the loan F they have to repay. Denote by $G(F)$ the distribution function. To derive an explicit example of a supply function, we simplify by assuming that monetary costs are quadratic, i.e. $c_1(n) = \frac{1}{2}\alpha n^2$ and effort costs are linear, i.e. $c_2(n) = \beta n$.

Now we are now in a position to derive the explicit values of $\underline{F}(p)$ and $\bar{F}(p)$. For small F, the physician sets price equal to marginal cost. Therefore $p = \alpha n + \beta$ and consequently

$$n^*(p) = \frac{p - \beta}{\alpha}. \tag{C.2}$$

He can do so, as long as his monetary income covers his loan. Therefore, $\underline{F}(p)$ is defined by $pn^*(p) - \frac{1}{2}\alpha(n^*(p))^2 = \underline{F}$, which implies

$$\underline{F} = \frac{p^2 - \beta^2}{2\alpha} \tag{C.3}$$

For values of F larger than $\underline{F}$ but not too large, the physician will work to avoid bankruptcy. This implies for the number of treatments $pn - \frac{1}{2}\alpha n^2 - F =$

0 and therefore

$$n(p, F) = \frac{1}{\alpha}[p - \sqrt{p^2 - 2\alpha F}] \qquad (C.4)$$

It directly follows that $n(p, F)$ decreases in p and increases in F. $\bar{F}$ can now be derived. As discussed in Section 4.2, there are two possible reasons why a physician might declare bankruptcy: Either the price exceeds monetary marginal costs or effort costs exceeds bankruptcy cost.

1.) In the first case, $p = \alpha n(p; \bar{F})$, which gives $\sqrt{p^2 - 2\alpha\bar{F}} = 0$ and therefore

$$\bar{F} = \frac{p^2}{2\alpha} \qquad (C.5)$$

2.) In the second case, $BK = \beta n(p, \bar{F})$, which gives $BK = \beta\frac{p}{\alpha} - \frac{\beta}{\alpha}\sqrt{p^2 - 2\alpha F}$ and therefore:

$$\bar{F} = \frac{1}{2}\alpha[p^2 - (p - \frac{\alpha}{\beta}BK)^2] = \frac{BK}{\beta}[p - \frac{\alpha}{2\beta}] \qquad (C.6)$$

Note that the second case is relevant if $\frac{p}{\alpha} > \frac{BK}{\beta}$.

Now we are able to derive the aggregate supply $N(p)$:

$$N(p) = \int_0^\infty n^*(p, F)dG(F) = G(\underline{F}) \cdot \frac{p - \beta}{\alpha} + \frac{1}{\alpha}\int_{\underline{F}}^{\bar{F}} (p - \sqrt{p^2 - 2\alpha F})dG(F) \qquad (C.7)$$

For our numerical example, we assume in addition that F is distributed uniformly on $[0, \hat{F}]$. By using the following values: $\alpha = 1$, $\beta = 8$, $\hat{F} = 8,5$ and BK large enough, a supply curve is obtained which is partly downward sloping. The curve is shown in Figure C.1.

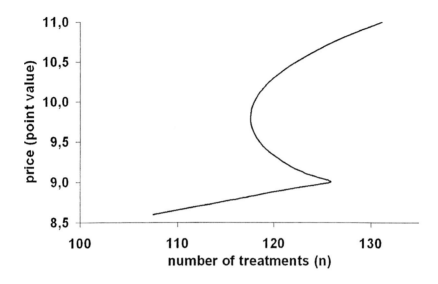

Figure C.1: Market Supply Curve

Appendix D

Appendix of Chapter 5

D.1 Proof of the Proposition for any Symmetric Distribution

In the following we proof that the proposition continues to holds for any symmetric distribution.

We again compare both schemes, the price system with the point system:

$$E[U(p\tilde{y} - c\tilde{y})] \succ \text{ or } \prec E[U(p\bar{y} - c\tilde{y})]$$

It is useful to define the wealth levels as new parameters: $z_1 = (p - c)\tilde{y}$ and $z_2 = p\bar{y} - c\tilde{y}$.

For any $\hat{z}$ and with $p > c$ it holds:
Price-system (F_1): $P(z_1 \leq \hat{z}) = P(\tilde{y} \leq \frac{\hat{z}}{p-c})$
Point-system (F_2): $P(z_2 \leq \hat{z}) = P(\tilde{y} \geq \frac{p\bar{y}-\hat{z}}{c})$.

Because of symmetry, it follows that $P(\tilde{y} \geq \frac{p\bar{y}-\hat{z}}{c}) = P(\tilde{y} \leq 2\bar{y} - \frac{p\bar{y}-\hat{z}}{c})$.
Therefore $P(z_1 \leq \hat{z}) < P(z_2 \leq \hat{z})$, if

$$\frac{\hat{z}}{p-c} < 2\bar{y} + \frac{\hat{z}}{c} - \frac{p}{c}\bar{y}. \tag{D.1}$$

To show that the distribution 1 second order stochastically dominates distribution 2 it is sufficient to show that for all values of $\hat{z}$ smaller than the average, F_1 is smaller than F_2, while it is the reverse for larger values. If we rewrite $\hat{z} = (p-c)\hat{y}$, inequality D.1 transforms to:

$$\bar{y}(2c-p) > \hat{y}(2c-p)$$

Therefore, if $p-c < c$ the inequality holds as long as $\hat{y} < \bar{y}$, which proves that the price system (F_1) dominates the point system (F_2). The reverse holds for $p-c > c$.

Q.E.D.

Appendix E

Glossary

German to English

German name	German abbreviation	English name
1. GKV-Neuverordnungsgesetz		First Statutory Health Insurance Restructuring Act
2. GKV-Neuverordnungsgesetz		Second Statutory Health Insurance Restructuring Act
Ärztekammer		(Regional) Physicians' Chamber
Allgemeine Ortskrankenkassen	AOK	General Regional Sickness Funds
Betriebskrankenkassen	BKK	Employees' Sickness Funds (Company-Based Sickness Funds)
Bewertungsausschuss		Valuation Committee
Bundesausschuss der Ärzte und Krankenkassen		Federal Committee of Physicians and Sickness Funds

Continued on the next page

Continued from the previous page

German to English

German name	German abbreviation	English name
Bundesknappschaft (Knappschaftliche Kranken-versicherung)		Federal Miners' Insurance Fund
Bundesministerium für Gesundheit	BMG	Federal Ministry of Health
Deutsche Krankenhaus-Gesell-schaft	DKG	German Hospital Organization
Einheitlicher Bewertungsmaß-stab	EBM	Uniform Value Standard (Uniform Value Scale)
Ersatzkassen		Substitute Insurance Funds
Fachärzte		Specialist Physicians
Gesetz zur Stärkung der Solidarität in der Gesetzlichen Krankenversicherung		Act to Strengthen Solidarity in Statutory Health Insurance
Gesetzliche Krankenversicherung	GKV	Statutory Health Insurance Funds (SHI) (include the Primary and Substitute Funds)
Gesundheitsreformgesetz	GRG	Health Care Reform Act 1989
Gesundheitsstrukturgesetz	GSG	Health Care Structure Act 1993
GKV-Gesundheitsreform 2000		Reform Act of SHI 2000
Grundgesetz		Basic Law (= Constitution)

Continued on the next page

Continued from the previous page

German to English

German name	German abbreviation	English name
Honorarverteilungsmaßstab	HVM	Remuneration Distribution Standard (Scale)
Innungskrankenkassen	IKK	Guild Sickness Funds
Kassenärztliche Bundesvereinigung	KBV	Federal Association of Panel Doctors (SIH Physicians)
Kassenärztliche Vereinigung	KV	(Regional) Association of Panel Doctors (Physicians' Association)
Kassenzahnärztliche Bundesvereinigung	KZBV	Federal Association of SHI Dentists
Kassenzahnärztliche Vereinigung	KZV	(Regional) Dentists' Association
Konzertierte Aktion im Gesundheitswesen	KAiG	Concerted Action in Health Care
Koordinierungsausschuss		Coordinating Committee (between Committee for Hospital Care and Federal Committee of Physicians and Sickness Funds)
Krankenversicherung		Health Insurance
Krankenversicherungskosten-dämpfungsgesetz	KVKG	Health Insurance Cost-Containment Act
Land (plural: Länder)		State(s)

Continued on the next page

Continued from the previous page

German to English

German name	German abbreviation	English name
Landwirtschaftliche Kranken-kassen	LKK	Farmers' Sickness Funds
Leistungserbringer		Providers
Primärkassen		Primary Funds
Sachverständigenrat (für die Konzertierte Aktion im Gesundheitswesen)	SVR	Advisory Council (of the Concerted Action in Health Care)
Seekrankenkasse		Sailors' Sickness Fund
Sozialgesetzbuch V	SGB V	Fifth Book of the Social Security Code (main body of German health care legislation)
Statistisches Bundesamt		Federal Statistical Office
Verband der privaten Kranken-versicherung	PKV	Association of Private Health Insurance
Vermittlungsausschuss		Arbitration Committee (between Federal Assembly and Federal Council)

English to German

English name	German name	German abbreviation
Act to Strengthen Solidarity in Statutory Health Insurance	Gesetz zur Stärkung der Solidarität in der Gesetzlichen Krankenversicherung	
Advisory Council (of the Concerted Action in Health Care)	Sachverständigenrat für die Konzertierte Aktion im Gesundheitswesen	(SVR)
Arbitration Committee (between Federal Assembly and Federal Council)	Vermittlungsausschuss	
Association of Private Health Insurance	Verband der privaten Kranken-versicherung	PKV
Authorities in charge of running healthcare institutions; this group includes, but is not limited to state, municipal, university or church-affiliated groups; "Kostenträger" refers explicitly to the payors (literally: "carriers" and "cost carriers")	Träger, Kostenträger	
Basic Law (= Constitution)	Grundgesetz	
Concerted Action in Health Care	Konzertierte Aktion im Gesundheitswesen	KAiG

Continued on the next page

Continued from the previous page

English to German

English name	German name	German abbreviation
Coordinating Committee (between Committee for Hospital Care and Federal Committee of Physicians and Sickness Funds)	Koordinierungsausschuss	
(Regional) Dentists' Association	Kassenzahnärztliche Vereinigung	KZV
Employees' Sickness Funds (Company-Based Sickness Funds)	Betriebskrankenkassen	BKK
Farmers' (Sickness) Funds	Landwirtschaftliche Krankenkassen	LKK
Federal Association of SHI Dentists	Kassenzahnärztliche Bundesvereinigung	KZBV
Federal Association of Panel Doctors (SIH Physicians)	Kassenärztliche Bundesvereinigung	KBV
Federal Committee of Physicians and Sickness Funds	Bundesausschuss für Ärzte und Krankenkassen	
Federal Ministry of Health	Bundesministerium für Gesundheit	BMG
Federal Miners' Insurance Fund	Bundesknappschaft (Knappschaftliche Krankenversicherung)	
Federal Statistical Office	Statistisches Bundesamt	

Continued on the next page

Continued from the previous page

English to German

English name	German name	German abbreviation
First Statutory Health Insurance Restructuring Act	1. GKV-Neuordnungsgesetz	
General Patients' Association	Allgemeiner Patienten-Verband	
General Regional Funds	Allgemeine Ortskrankenkassen	AOK
Guild (Sickness) Funds	Innungskrankenkassen	IKK
Health Care Reform Act 1989	Gesundheitsreformgesetz	GRG
Health Care Structure Act 1993	Gesundheitsstrukturgesetz	GSG
Health Insurance Contribution Rate Exoneration Act	Krankenversicherungsbeitrags-entlastungsgesetz	
Health Insurance Cost-Containment Act	Krankenversicherungskosten-dämpfungsgesetz	KVKG
Income Limit for the Assessment of Contributions (effect: poeple earning above the limit do not have to pay higher contributions)	Beitragsbemessungsgrenze	
Labor´s share in national income (i.e., quotient of total wage bill and national income or: of average real wage rate and labor productivity)	gesamtwirtschaftliche Lohn-summe, Grundlohnsumme	

Continued on the next page

Continued from the previous page

English to German

English name	German name	German abbreviation
Organization of German Primary Care Physicians - General Practitioners' Union	Berufsverband der Allgemein-ärzte Deutschlands - Hausärzte-verband	
Pharmaceuticals Budget, Drug Budget	Arzneimittelbudget	
Primary Funds	Primärkassen	
Providers	Leistungserbringer	
(Regional) Association of Panel Doctors (Physicians' Association)	Kassenärztliche Vereinigung	KV
Reform Act of SHI 2000	GKV-Gesundheitsreform 2000	
Remuneration Distribution Standard (Scale)	Honorarverteilungsmaßstab	HVM
Sailors' (Sickness) Fund	Seekrankenkasse	
Second Statutory Health Insurance Restructuring Act	2. GKV-Neuordnungsgesetz	
Social Code Book V (statutory Health Insurance)	Sozialgesetzbuch V	SGB V
Specialist Physicians	Fachärzte	
State(s)	Land (plural: Länder)	

Continued on the next page

Continued from the previous page

English to German

English name	German name	German abbreviation
Statutory Health Insurance (SHI)	Gesetzlichekrankenversicherung	GKV
Substitute Insurance Funds	Ersatzkassen	
Uniform Evaluation Standard (Uniform Value Standard)	Einheitlicher Bewertungsmaß-stab	EBM
Valuation Committee	Bewertungsausschuss	

Bibliography

ADVISORY COUNCIL FOR THE CONCERTED ACTION IN HEALTH CARE (1997): *The Health Care System in Germany - Cost Factor and Branch of the Future (Special Report)*, vol. II: Progress and Growth Markets, Finance and Remuneration. Bonn, see for the German version Sachverständigenrat für die Konzertierte Aktion im Gesundheitswesen (1997).

ALTENSTETTER, C. (1999): "From Solidarity to Market Competition? Values, Structure, and Strategy in German Health Care Policy 1883 - 1997," in *Health Care Systems in Transition*, ed. by F. D. Powell, and A. Wessen, pp. 47–88. SAGE Publications, Thousand Oaks, London and New Delhi.

ARROW, K. J. (1963): "Uncertainty and the Welfare Economics of Medical Care," *American Economic Review*, 53, 941–973.

ÄRZTE-ZEITUNG (1996): "Korrekturen bringen die Punktwerte wieder klar auf über sieben Pfennig.," July, 3.

AUSTER, R. D., AND R. O. OAXACA (1981): "Identification of Supplier Induced Demand in the Health Care Sector," *Journal of Human Resources*, 16, 327–342.

BARER, M., R. J. LABELLE, S. MORRIS, R. EVANS, AND G. STODDART (1978): "The Impact on Medical Service Utilization of British Columbia's 1982/1983 Physician Fee 'Giveback'," *Canadian Journal of Public Health*, 87, 37–42.

BERLINER MORGENPOST (1997): "Kassenärzte warnen vor Pleitewelle," October, 19.

——— (1999): "Der Dr. med garantiert in Deutschland keinen Job mehr," June, 24.

BIRCH, S. (1988): "The Identification of Supplier-Inducement in a Fixed Price System of Health Care Provision," *Journal of Health Economics*, 7, 129–150.

BREYER, F. (2000): "Zukunftsperspektiven der Gesundheitssicherung," in *Beiheft 8: Die Zukunft Des Sozialstaats*, pp. 167–199. Zeitschrift für Wirtschafts- und Sozialwissenschaften.

BUNDESGESETZBLATT (1988): "Gesetz zur Strukturreform im Gesundheitswesen (Gesundheits-Reformgesetz - GRG) vom 29.12.1988," Bonn.

——— (1992): "Gesetz zur Sicherung und Strukturverbesserung der gesetzlichen Krankenversicherung (Gesundheitsstrukturgesetz) vom 21.12.1992," Bonn.

——— (1997a): "Erstes Gesetz zur Neuordnung von Selbstverwaltung und Eigenverantwortung in der gesetzlichen Krankenversicherung (1. GKV-Neuordnungsgesetz - 1. NOG) vom 30.6.1997," Bonn.

——— (1997b): "Zweites Gesetz zur Neuordnung von Selbstverwaltung und Eigenverantwortung in der gesetzlichen Krankenversicherung (2. GKV-Neuordnungsgesetz - 2. NOG) vom 30.6.1997," Bonn.

BUNDESMINISTERIUM FÜR GESUNDHEIT (2000a): "Eckpunkte zur Gesundheitsreform 2000," Bonn.

——— (2000b): "Informationen zum Gesetz zur Reform der gesetzlichen Krankenversicherung ab dem Jahr 2000 (GKV-Gesundheitsreform 2000),"

.

——— (2000c): *Statistisches Taschenbuch Gesundheit 2000*. Bonn.

CARLSEN, F., AND J. GRYTTEN (1998): "More Physicians: Improved Availability or Induce Demand?," *Health Economics*, 7, 495–508.

CROMWELL, J., AND J. B. MITCHELL (1988): "Physician Induced Demand for Surgery," *Journal of Health Economics*, 18, 407–424.

DARBY, M. R., AND E. KARNI (1973): "Free Competition and the Optimal Amount of Fraud," *Journal of Law and Economics*, 16, 67–88.

DEUTSCHES ÄRZTEBLATT (1997): "Rückgang der Praxisüberschüsse," 49, A–3361.

DIE ZEIT (2000): "Das Krankenhaus der Zukunft," August, 31.

DOMENIGHETTI, G., A. CASABIACA, F. GUTZWILLER, AND S. MARTINOLLI (1993): "Revisiting the Most Informed Consumer of Surgical Services," *International Journal of Technology Assessment in Health Care*, 9, 505–513.

DRANOVE, D. (1988): "Demand Inducement and the Physician/Patient Relationship," *Economic Inquiry*, 26, 281–298.

DRANOVE, D., AND P. WEHNER (1994): "Physician-Induced Demand for Childbirths," *Journal of Health Economics*, 13, 61–73.

DRANOVE, D., AND W. D. WHITE (1987): "Agency and the Organization of Health Care Delivery," *Inquiry*, 24, 405–415.

ELLIS, R. P., AND T. G. MCGUIRE (1986): "Provider Behaviour under Prospective Reimbursement," *Journal of Health Economics*, 5(2), 129–151.

——— (1990): "Optimal Payment Systems for Health Services," *Journal of Health Economics*, 4, 375–396.

——— (1993): "Supply-Side and Demand-Side Cost Sharing in Health Care," *Journal of Economic Perspectives*, 7, 135–151.

EMONS, W. (1997): "Credence Goods and Fraudulent Experts," *RAND Journal of Economics*, 28, 107–119.

ESCARCE, J. (1992): "Explaining the Association Between Surgeon Supply and Utilization," *Inquiry*, 29(4), 403–415.

EUROPEAN OBSERVATORY ON HEALTH CARE SYSTEMS (2000): *Health Care Systems in Transition (Germany)*. WHO Regional Office for Europe, Kopenhagen.

EVANS, R. A. (1974): "Supplier-Induced Demand: Some Empirical Evidence and Implications," in *The Economics of Health and Medical Care*, ed. by M. Perlman. MacMillan, London.

FEDERAL ASSOCIATION OF PANEL DOCTORS (1999): *Statistics of Outpatient Care in Germany (Grunddaten zur Kassenärztlichen Versorgung in der Bundesrepublik Deutschland)*. Deutscher Ärzte-Verlag, Köln, (Kassenärztliche Bundesvereinigung).

FELDMAN, R., AND F. SLOAN (1988): "Competition Among Physicians, Revisited," *Journal of Health Politics, Policy and Law*, 13, 239–261.

——— (1989): "Reply from Feldman and Sloan," *Journal of Health Politics*, 14.

FUCHS, V. R. (1978): "The Supply of Surgeons and the Demand for Operations," *Journal of Human Resources*, 13 (supplement), 35–56.

GAYNOR, M. (1994): "Issues in the Industrial Organization of the Market for Physician Services," *Journal of Economics & Management Strategy*, 3(1), 211–255.

GAYNOR, M., AND D. HAAS-WILSON (1999): "Change, Consolidation, and Competition in Health Care Markets," *Journal-of-Economic-Perspectives*, 13(1), 141–164.

GRUBER, J., AND M. OWINGS (1996): "Physician Financial Incentives and Cesarean Section Delivery," *RAND Journal of Economics*, 27, 99–123.

GRYTTEN, J., F. CARLSEN, AND R. SORENSEN (1995): "Supplier Inducement in a Public Health Care System," *Journal of Health Economics*, 14(2), 207–229.

GRYTTEN, J., D. HOLST, AND P. LAAKE (1990): "Supplier Inducement: Its Effects on Dental Services in Norway.," *Journal of Health Economics*, 9, 483–491.

HANDELSBLATT (1999): "Ärzte haben kein Rezept gegen den Misserfolg," September 9, 1999.

HARSANYI, J., AND R. SELTEN (1988): *A General Theory of Equilibrium Selection in Games*. MIT Press, Cambridge, Mass.

HAY, J., AND M. LEAHY (1982): "Physician-Induced Demand: An Empirical Analysis of the Information Gap," *Journal of Health Economics*, 3, 231–244.

HICKSON, G. B., W. A. ALTMEIER, AND J. M. PERRIN (1987): "Physician Reimbursement by Salary of Fee-For-Service-Effect on Physician Practice Behavior in a Randomized Prospective Study," *Pediatrics*, 80, 344–350.

HOLAHAN, J., AND W. SCANLON (1978): *Price Controls, Physician Fees, and Physician Incomes from Medicare and Medicaid*. The Urban Institute, Washington, D.C.

HURLEY, J., AND R. CARD (1996): "Global Physician Budgets as Common-Property Resources: Some Implications for Physicians and Medical Associations," *Can Ned Assoc J*, 154, 1161–1168.

HURLEY, J., R. J. LABELLE, AND T. H. RICE (1990): "The Relationship Between Physician Fees and the Utilization of Medical Sercies in Ontario," *Advances in Health Economics and Health Services Research*, 11, 49–78.

HWWA - INSTITUT FÜR WIRTSCHAFTSFORSCHUNG (1999): "Zeitge-spräch zur Gesundheitsreform 2000," *Wirtschaftsdienst - Zeitschrift für Wirtschaftspolitik*, 79, 207–224.

HYPOVEREINSBANK (1998): "Branchenreport Ärzte," .

——— (1999): "Branchenreport Zahnärzte," .

KANAVOS, P., AND J. YFANTOPOULOS (1999): "Cost Containment and Health Expenditure in the EU: A Macroeconomic Perspective," in *Health Care and Cost Containment in the European Union*, ed. by E. Mossialos, and J. Le Grand, chap. 2, pp. 155–196. Ashgate, Aldershot, Brookfield (USA) et al.

KASSENÄRZTLICHE VEREINIGUNG BAYERNS (1998): "Modellvorhaben Gesundheitsförderung von Kassenärztlicher Vereinigung Bayerns und AOK Bayern – Neue Beratungsangebote in Gesundheitsförderung und Prävention," Presseinformation vom 8. September 1998.

KENKEL, D. (1990): "Consumer Health Information and the Demand for Medical Care," *Review of Economics and Statistics*, 72, 587–595.

KRASNIK, A., P. GROENEWEGEN, P. A. PEDERSEN, P. SCHOLTEN, G. MOONEY, A. GOTTSCHAU, H. FLIERMAN, AND M. T. DAMSGAARD (1990): "Changing Remuneration Systems: Effects on Activity in General Practice," *British Medical Journal*, 300, 1698–1701.

LABELLE, R. J., G. STODDART, AND T. H. RICE (1994): "A Re-Examination of the Meaning and Importance of Supplier-Induced Demand," *Journal of Health Economics*, 13, 347–368.

LEITER, J. M. E., H. LOEST, AND C. THIELSCHER (1997): "Managed Care – Ansätze zur Weiterentwicklung des deutschen Gesundheitswesens," in *Reformstategie "Managed Care"*, ed. by E. Knappe. Baden-Baden.

MA, C.-T., AND T. G. MCGUIRE (1997): "Optimal Health Insurance and Provider Payment," *American Economic Review*, 87, 685–704.

MCGUIRE, T. G., AND M. V. PAULY (1992): "Physician Responses to Fee Changes with Multiple Payers," *Journal of Health Economics*, 10, 385–410.

MITCHELL, J. B., AND M. L. ROSENBACH (1989): "Feasibility of Case-Based Payment for Inpatient Radiology, Anesthesia, and Pathology Services," *Inquiry*, 26, 457–467.

NEWHOUSE, J. E. (1992): "Pricing and Imperfections in the Medical Care Marketplace," in *Health Economics Worldwide*, ed. by H. E. Frech III, and P. Zweifel. Dordrecht: Kluwer Academic.

OECD (2000): *OECD Health Data 2000 – A Comparative Analysis Of 29 Countries*.

PAULY, M. V. (1968): "The Economics of Moral Harzard," *American Economic Review*, 58, 231–237.

PHELPS, C. E. (1986): "Induced Demand. Can We Ever Know its Extent? Editorial," *Journal of Health Economics*, 5, 355–365.

PITCHIK, C., AND A. SCHOTTER (1987): "Honesty in a Model of Strategic Information Transmission," *American Economic Review*, 77, 1032–1036.

RAMSEY, J. B., AND B. WASOW (1986): "Supplier Induced Dmeand for Physician Services: Theoretical Anomaly or Statistical Artifact? An Econometric Evaluation of some Important Models in Physician Service Markets.," *Advances in Econometrics*, 5, 49–77.

REINHARDT, U. E. (1978): "Parkinsons's Law and the Demand for Physician Services," in *Competition in the Health Care Sector: Past, Present, and Future*, ed. by G. L., and W. Greenberg. Federal Trade Commission, Washington, D.C.

——— (1985): "The Theory of Physician-Induced Demand. Reflections After a Decade," *Journal of Health Economics*, 4, 187–193.

——— (1989): "Economists in Health Care: Saviors, or Elephants in a Porcelain Shop?," *Amercian-Economic-Review*, 79, 337–342.

RICE, T. H. (1983): "Physician-Induced Demand for Medical Care: New Evidence from the Medicare Program," *Advances in Health Economics and Health Services Research*, pp. 129–160.

RICE, T. H., AND R. J. LABELLE (1989): "Do Physicians Induce Demand for Medical Services," *Journal of Health Politics, Policy and Law*, 14, 587–600.

ROEMER, M. I. (1961): "Bed Supply and Hospital Utilization: A National Experiment," *Hospitals*, 35, 36–42.

ROSSITER, L. F., AND G. R. WILENSKY (1983): "A Reexamination of the Use of Physician Services: The Role of Physician Induced Demand," *Inquiry*, 20, 162–172.

ROTHSCHILD, M., AND J. STIGLITZ (1970): "Increasing Risk I: A Definition," *Journal of Economic Theory*, 2, 225–43.

SACHVERSTÄNDIGENRAT FÜR DIE KONZERTIERTE AKTION IM GESUNDHEITSWESEN (1997): *Gesundheitswesen in Deutschland: Kostenfaktor und Zukunftsbranche (Sondergutachten)*, vol. II: Fortschritt und Wachstumsmärkt , Finanzierung und Vergütung. Nomos, Baden-Baden, see for the English version Advisory Council for the Concerted Action in Health Care (1997).

SCHMIDT, K. M. (1997): "Managerial Incentives and Product Market Competition," *Review of Economic Studies*, 64, 191–214.

SCOTT, A., AND J. HALL (1995): "Evaluating the Effects of GP Remuneration: Problems and Prospects," *Health Policy*, 31, 183–195.

SHAIN, M., AND M. ROEMER (1959): "Hospital Costs Relate to the Supply of Beds," *modern hospital*, pp. 71–79.

SÜDDEUTSCHE ZEITUNG (2000): "Immer mehr Kassenärzte lassen Patienten finanziell zur Ader," 11.4.2000.

THIEMEYER, T. (1985): "Honorierungsprobleme in der Bundesrepublik Deutschland (Arzteinkommen, Steuerungsprobleme Usw.)," in *Kosten und Effizienz im Gesundheitswesen*, ed. by H. von Ferber, U. E. R. ., and H. Schaefer, pp. 35–58. Oldenbourg, München.

TUSSING, A. D. (1983): "Physician Induced Demand for Medical Care: Irish General Practitioners," *Economic and Social Review*, 23, 225–247.

TUSSING, A. D., AND M. J. WOJTOWYCZ (1986): "Physician Induced Demand by Irish GPs," *Social Science and Medicine*, 23, 851–860.

VERBAND DER PRIVATEN KRANKENVERSICHERUNG E.V. (2000): *Die Private Krankenversicherung: Rechenschaftsbericht 1999*. Verband der privaten Krankenversicherung e.V., Koeln.

WEISBROD, B. A. (1991): "The Health Care Quadrilemma: An Essay on Technological Change, Insurance, Quality of Care and Cost-Containment," *Journal of Economic Literature*, 29(2), 523–552.

WOLINSKY, A. (1993): "Competition in the Market for Informed Expert Services," *RAND Journal of Economics*, 24, 380–398.

——— (1995): "Competition in Markets for Credence Goods," *Journal of Institutional and Theoretical Economics*, 151, 117–131.

ZECKHAUSER, R. (1970): "Medical Insurance: A Case Study of the Tradeoff Between Risk Spreading and Appropriate Incentives.," *Journal of Economic Theory*, 1, 10–26.

ZENTRALINSTITUT (1988-1998): "Die Kostenstrukturanalyse für die Kassenärztliche Versorgung in der Bundesrepublik Deutschland," .

Peter Lang · Europäischer Verlag der Wissenschaften

Manfred Albring / Eberhard Wille (Hrsg.)

Qualitätsorientierte Vergütungssysteme in der ambulanten und stationären Behandlung

Frankfurt/M., Berlin, Bern, Bruxelles, New York, Oxford, Wien, 2001. 280 S., zahlr. Abb. und Tab.
Allokation im marktwirtschaftlichen System. Bd. 44
Verantwortlicher Herausgeber: Eberhard Wille
ISBN 3-631-38314-2 · br. DM 56.– / € 28.60*

Der Sammelband enthält die erweiterten Referate eines interdisziplinären Workshops über qualitätsorientierte Vergütungssysteme in der ambulanten und stationären Behandlung. Diskutiert werden die vier Themenkreise Priorisierung von Gesundheitszielen, Vergütungssysteme im ambulanten Bereich, Vergütungssysteme im stationären Bereich sowie integrierte Versorgungsformen. Der Teilnehmerkreis setzt sich aus Vertretern der Ärzteschaft, Krankenkassen und -versicherungen, der pharmazeutischen Industrie, der Wissenschaft, der ministerialen Bürokratie und der Politik zusammen.

Frankfurt/M · Berlin · Bern · Bruxelles · New York · Oxford · Wien
Auslieferung: Verlag Peter Lang AG
Jupiterstr. 15, CH-3000 Bern 15
Telefax (004131) 9402131

*inklusive der in Deutschland gültigen Mehrwertsteuer
Preisänderungen vorbehalten

Homepage http://www.peterlang.de